Showdown at Shinagawa

You will step on the soil of many
countries in your lifetime.

SHOWDOWN
at
SHINAGAWA

Tales of Filming from Bombay to Brazil

BILL ZARCHY

Roving
Camera
Press

Albany | California

Showdown at Shinagawa: Tales of Filming from Bombay to Brazil

Library of Congress Control Number: 2013919732

ROVING CAMERA PRESS
Bill Zarchy, Publisher

Visit *Showdown* online for videos and more photos—
showdownatshinagawa.com
Facebook Page—facebook.com/showdownatshinagawa

Email—billzarchy@gmail.com
Director of Photography site—billzarchy.com
Roving Camera Blog—billzarchy.com/blog

Book and cover design by Maggie Hurley
Inside author photo by Toshihiro Oshima, Tokyo 2008
Front cover photos:
Top (Ramen bar)—Bill Zarchy, Tokyo 2011
Bottom (Kiyomizu temple)—Rod Williams, Kyoto 1993
Back cover photos (paperback only):
Top (Bus station ladies)—Bill Zarchy, Mandaya, Karnataka, India 2005
Author—Roel Tanghe, Bruges 2010

ISBN: 978-0-9849191-0-9 (paperback)
ISBN: 978-0-9849191-1-6 (e-book)

For Pop

Who taught me, by example,
how to be a writer, a father, and a man.

Contents

Contents

Introduction
Larry Habegger

One of the first stories I ever read from Bill Zarchy was "Showdown at Shinagawa," the title track of this book, and I remember at the time marveling at how he could transform a blue-collar sport like bowling into a cultural crossroads. About the same time I read "Wrecks and Pissers," and I remember thinking that he was just about to run off the figurative road when, with a deft change of tone, he righted himself and made me smile.

From then on I looked forward to whatever he presented to our writers group, Townsend ii, because his stories were always entertaining, often thoughtful, usually informative, and invariably a pleasure to read.

Bill's writing has the quality of a warm beverage on a cold day: smooth, comforting, welcoming. Reading his work makes you feel you're engaged in a conversation, that he's talking to you and bringing you into his world and gauging your responses. His words flow, his stories build, and before you know it you're laughing along with him or feeling his pain.

In this volume of tales about his filming experiences around the world, Bill takes us along behind the scenes of international film production. Everywhere he turns he encounters cultural illuminations or obstacles (sometimes literal ones, as in his story, "Singapore: No Worry, Chicken Curry," where he takes his six-foot-four frame into a land of more Lilliputian proportions, or in "Gigantic in Japan," when a restroom's low doorway knocks him flat). He learns how compromising it can be to live a lie in New Zealand, how challenging the true face of globalization is in Hong Kong, and just how far he should push to accommodate a client in a Tokyo high-rise.

Most people know that the film world isn't all glamour, and Bill doesn't gloss over the difficulties in getting what the crew needs. Boredom can be a regular companion, but they always find a way to manage it. How? By playing games. "Wrecks and Pissers" is just that, an impromptu game to endure an interminable ride on one of India's most dangerous roads.

The consequences are unpredictable but the lesson worthwhile. The "Showdown at Shinagawa" begins as a way to bond with each other and their clients but turns into a fierce competition and a surprising cultural tonic. And in "Brazil: Some Days the Bear Eats You," we learn how to manage when things just don't work out.

What about the challenges of getting the job done when you have to improvise? In Taiwan, he reveals the importance of an effective local connection and knowing how to speak the same language, even when you don't. In China, during his "Shanghai Lunch," we see the importance of clear communication, even when you have a fixer. And in "The Big Break: Malaise in Manila," he takes on a huge shoot outside his comfort zone at a crucial time in his career and wonders, could this be the break he was looking for?

But it's not all fun and games. "21st-Century Village: Telemedicine in Rural India," and "Uganda: A World Together" inspire us with what one person can do to make the world a better place. "Health: Our Most Important Product" draws moving portraits of medical patients that help us see past the corporate sponsors or medical products. "Steve Jobs: Consuming the Apples" gives us a sneak peak into the first Apple Store and the Apple founder's genius.

Bill's stories are peopled with characters, whether his production team cronies, the subjects of their shoots, local hires, or people met along the way. Bill brings them all to life and treats them fairly, allowing us to enjoy their company or sympathize with the difficulties they face. He even makes a personal connection with Bill Clinton over the loss of their dogs.

In the end he brings it all home. During a brief moment of glamour in Cannes he finds a familiar face in the crowd, and when he's working a tedious job in Shenyang, China, a hotel house band of Filipino entertainers plays his crew a special tune to ease their homesickness. Never mind that it's far off the mark, the point is that people the world over care about each other and find ways to connect.

Bill shows us how, behind the scenes.

Showdown at Shinagawa:
Bowling for Budget in Tokyo

On our first night in Japan, Randy dragged us up the hill behind our hotel to go bowling.

Shinagawa Lanes was an electronic wonder attached to the Shinagawa Prince, a large hotel tower with tiny rooms where Randy had stayed on his first visit to Japan years before.

Little did we know that this would be the eventual setting for an epic bowling challenge with our clients.

Shinagawa featured more than 100 lanes, each with a video monitor and two hidden TV cameras. The monitor first showed you bowling on your lane, then switched to the ball hitting the pins. After each frame, the system displayed your name, score, and the speed of your last ball in kilometers per hour. On unoccupied lanes, the monitors played Japanese music videos of all kinds, from darkly-tanned, red-haired Asian rappers and hip-hop dancers, to boy bands, Spice-Girl-like girl bands, and one video with two young men crooning romantically to each other and kissing at the end of the song.

It was light years away from the homey 1950s ambience of the bowling alley near my home in California. I was used to a different crowd, a multi-racial, casually dressed mix of old-timers, students, and young families. These Japanese bowlers looked prosperous—men in suits with faces red from alcohol, young girls and guys in nice outfits one might wear to the office. We were the only foreigners.

The four of us arrived about 8:30, to bowl three games each. They weren't very busy. The clerk bowed, smiled, and suggested we bowl league-style, alternating on two lanes. That way, he explained painstakingly, we would finish by their 10 p.m. closing time. We politely declined. Our bowling was rusty, and we preferred a slower pace on one lane. The clerk then went through the kind of neuro-lingual lockup I sometimes see in Japanese who fluster that they are not being understood, that their English has suddenly failed them.

Rattled, the clerk called a manager, who explained carefully, "It is better for you to bowl on two lanes, so we can close at 10 o'clock."

"We understand," said Randy, "but we prefer one lane. Don't worry, we'll be done in time." So we rented shoes, found balls, and started to bowl.

At about 9:30, the programming on the monitors near us stopped in the middle of a song by heavy metal Japanese headbangers, and CLOSING TIME 10 OCLOCK appeared in large block letters. We noticed then that we were the only customers still bowling on our half of Shinagawa Lanes. We hurried through our third games as maintenance crews oiled and polished the lanes all around us. We were out by 9:50, with thanks and bows, but Randy couldn't resist asking impishly, "Say, what time do you close?" They handed us a printout of our scores in Japanese, frame-by-frame and pin-by-pin, a fun memento to tape to the hotel room mirror.

We swooped down to the video arcade under the bowling alley, where we machine-gunned skeletal monsters, reeled in large-mouth bass, water-skied like champions, and drove big rigs down the Pacific Coast Highway in Santa Monica. Each game for 100 yen, about a buck. All the locations and evil people in these Japanese games looked distinctly American.

This inauspicious start to our epic bowling adventure came during my fourth stay at the Pacific Meridien Hotel, across from Shinagawa Station in central Tokyo. My first time there came in 1977, before it was part of the Meridien chain, as a young camera assistant on a rock-and-roll concert tour. Randy had never let me live that one down: "I know, the first time you stayed here was with Fleetwood Mac. Now you're here with me!"

More recently, we had stayed there several times while filming in Tokyo for the company, a major Japanese electronics manufacturer. The Pacific Meridien was just a mile down the street from their Super Tower.

The Meridien Hotel chain was French, and the decor was Continental, with caricatures of French people and Parisian scenes on the walls, on the hotel literature, and on the room cardkeys. Walking through the lobby elicited a constant stream of "hellosirs" and "goodmorningsirs" from smiling doormen, bellmen, desk personnel, managers, shop owners, chambermaids, supervisors, and maitre d's. None were French. Being that friendly tired me out. Most of the other guests were well-dressed European and Japanese businessmen, a few tourists, and Air France flight crews. I felt shabby in my jeans and LL Bean shirts.

Since our last visit, the pricy sashimi-and-sushi restaurant in the lower level had been replaced by a TGI Friday's. Young Japanese guys and gals, many sporting red hair, waited tables and tended bar in cowboy boots, vests, chaps, and pins that said "Ask Me About Curly Fries" or "Margaritas 450 Yen." Unlike many of the restaurants in the Shinagawa area, it featured cheap food (for Tokyo), late hours, a full bar, and casual cross-pollinated international atmosphere. One night we celebrated Larry's birthday there with burgers, fries, and beers. It was a big hit.

From the front door of the hotel, we could see two McDonald's. Because the breakfast buffet at the Pacific cost about half my per diem meal money, to break our fasts many mornings, we joined a silent parade of foreigners out the side door of the hotel, sharing the sidewalks with thronging commuters spewing from Shinagawa Station.

An Egg McMuffin Set, with coffee, orange juice and mini-slab of home fries cost about double what I'd pay for a Value Meal if I ever went to a stateside Mickey D's, but much less than the hotel breakfast. Another local place called Art Coffee—"That's gotta be someone's name," Jon insisted—featured Hum & Egg and Cranberry Scorn on the menu, two of my favorites.

Meanwhile, we had work to do. On this, my eighth trip to Japan, I was the director of photography and had logged many miles on many projects with Randy, our director, and Larry, our producer. Jon, our video and audio engineer, was still the new kid in our group, despite having proven himself on a trip earlier that year to Costa Rica, Alaska, and India. We had started in Bangkok, then flown in to Tokyo for a couple of weeks, to shoot a corporate project for the company. But our clients were proving difficult to work with.

In preparation for shooting the next week, we spent a day scouting locations with Carole—our fixer, the local Japanese producer we had hired to book our crew, rent equipment, make arrangements for filming, and make us understood in a language we didn't speak. We needed the clients to arrange for us to film interviews with engineers and marketing personnel from other companies, but getting them to commit to arrangements was an annoying process.

Waffling was their forte. Despite working insanely long hours, our clients were clearly errand boys with little authority. They were unwilling to make changes, decisions, or phone calls. Clearly some higher-up was really in charge.

On our scout day we surveyed several locations until 11, then had one place left, only a few blocks away. Our appointment was at 3.

"Let's call them and arrange to come early," said Larry. But our clients, typically, refused to try to move it up, or to let Carole or Larry call. I'm sure they felt that constantly resisting the impudent wishes of the pushy barbarian filmmakers was important to maintaining decorous relations with our subjects. They refused to rock the boat, or even tip it a bit. If we were expected in four hours, we would wait till then. This process frustrated us, but it was a beautiful day in Tokyo, so we walked around, ate lunch, chatted, window-shopped ... and arrived early.

Before my first visit years before, I had naively assumed that Japanese people, with their modern, technologically advanced culture, were much like Americans. Unlike the characters in *Seven Samurai* or *Rashomon*, the Kurosawa movies I saw in film school, they eschewed kimonos and sandals for Western dress, made great cars and electronics, commuted on trains, worked in skyscrapers, bought and emulated our music and styles, watched our movies. But cultural dissimilarities persisted despite similar styles, clothing, and technology. For us, calling on the day of an appointment to change the time was an inevitable consequence of the ad hoc, truncated time clock of filmmaking, a crazy business for sure. For them, it conveyed indecision and weakness and was just not appropriate.

"The world would be boring if we were all the same," I told Larry. But it might make this project easier.

After Bangkok, we had been scheduled to spend several days filming in Singapore. But the Singapore shoot fell through before we left the States. Rather than try to reschedule Bangkok, our clients had decided to bring us to Japan nearly a week early, with little to do.

So we had several days off in Tokyo, and the time went very slowly. We had seen the Imperial Palace, temples, and museums on earlier visits. Traditional culture in Japan was on the wane, and shopping was expensive. Movie admissions were costly, and didn't guarantee a seat. The hotel TVs ran a lot of Japanese movies, unsubtitled, and I could only stand so much CNN and BBC. When I realized I was watching a repeat of the same Larry King show I'd seen earlier, or a Spanish-Japanese language lesson, I ran out to the hotel bookstore to buy a new novel.

Our biggest distraction on that visit in December 2000 was the political circus in the U.S. The presidential election hung in the balance, and Bush and Gore were slugging it out in Florida courts, with a series of breathtakingly dramatic decisions. Counties recounted ballots, stopped recounting, restarted, and variously obeyed or ignored orders from Florida's Secretary of State. The brother of the Republican Presidential nominee was the governor of the most hotly disputed state in the closest election crisis in history, and no one seemed to think that was odd.

"Chad" invaded our vocabulary, referring to incomplete punch-outs hanging from the holes on punch-card ballots, which bewildered the automated vote counter machines. A confusing "butterfly ballot" was blamed for causing many Holocaust survivors in Palm Beach to vote for right-wing Holocaust questioner Pat Buchanan.

The inventor of the voting machine most widely used in the U.S. claimed it had an inaccuracy rate of ten percent. Ten percent? Had the world gone mad? It was odd and disorienting to be out of the country as this constitutional stew simmered on the front burner back home.

By the end of our first week in Tokyo, we had bowled three times. Randy and I were scoring regularly in the high 140s. Larry's bowling started off slowly but improved steadily. He and Jon hadn't bowled in years.

Randy shared his secret to bowling success: knock down more pins.

Great advice. Thanks for sharing.

Miraculously, in those first few bowling sessions, my ball twisted sharply to the left as it approached the pins, a welcome hook which had been absent from my game since my teenage bowling league days. This hook did, in fact, knock down more pins and cause more strikes.

We were improving. During our shoot the following week, out of the blue, Randy invited our three main clients to bowl with us. Only one of them showed up that evening, still dressed in suit and tie from work, and typed in Takk as his name on the bowling lane computer. I was flabbergasted. They addressed us by our first names, which we preferred, but for each other they used surnames with Mister, the occasional Miss, or the useful "-san," an honorific suffix for either gender. I didn't know any of their first names. After one game with Takk, who hadn't bowled in a while, I urged him to remove his tie. He tried it for a few frames, but his accuracy suffered, and he soon retied it. In all, we bowled and beered our way through five games, then bid goodnight to Takk and headed back down the hill to our hotel.

On our next shoot day, Takk was back to Mister, though we reminisced about our fun bowling. He never used his first name again, even when we bowled later with his colleagues from the company.

As the days passed, Larry and I befriended two cute young girls in prim white uniforms who worked at Mario's Gelato near our hotel. They enjoyed practicing their English, and we had fun chatting and kibitzing with them.

When we walked in after bowling, they would stop what they were doing, bow, smile broadly, and say, very slowly and formally, "Hello! It is very nice to see you here again. Thank you for returning once more to see us. How can we serve you?" and later "Where do you come from? I would like to go to San Francisco some day. How do you like Japan? How long will you be staying here in Tokyo? Are you here for business or pleasure?" I wondered if any of them would ever visit the U.S.

For our part, while they struggled valiantly to learn our language, we added constantly to our ongoing collection of Japanized English. A passenger in the hotel elevator wore a sweatshirt imprinted "Smudgy Decision," a subway ad for "armless headphones" touted "the mode of ears," and we heard of two well-known but discontinued products: a hair spray called "Blow Me" and a baby shampoo named "My Pee." Later, friends told us of "Poop Dick," a clothing store.

On earlier trips we had delighted in discovering an amusement park outside Tokyo called "Wonder Eggs 2," a car model called "We've," a produce delivery service in Kyoto named "Tomato Call," and a marquee in Tokyo that proclaimed, inexplicably, "Modern Hipsters" and "Nude Trump." Perhaps these were band names, we thought at the time (on another visit years later, I learned that Nude Trump was a vintage clothing line).

Worst of all, "Pocari Sweat" and "Calpis" were popular Japanese soft drinks, both incomprehensibly wrong to American ears.

The interviews (with our Sony F-900 high-definition camera) proceeded slowly. Toward the end of our shoot, Randy impulsively challenged our clients to a bowling match—double or nothing for the budget of the film. Of course it was a joke, because the bet involved hundreds of thousands of dollars, but we had enjoyed spending time with them outside of work, we were having fun bowling ... and we thought we could beat them.

"If we find all this so exciting," I said to Jon, "then clearly we've been on the road too long."

But the challenge was answered: on our penultimate night in Japan, three of our clients would face us on the lanes after dinner. The excitement grew as evening approached, egged on by an email from Jim, the writer for our film, back in San Francisco: "Good luck with the Showdown at Shinagawa. Try not to squander away the whole budget."

As we wrapped for the day, I was distracted by news that the U.S. Supreme Court had awarded the Presidency to Dubya Bush. The Court saw merit in Al Gore's challenges to the official, Republican-certified Bush victory in Florida, but they said too much time had gone by since the election, and a quick decision was vital. For the good of the nation, of course. CNN and BBC were filled with repetitive stories and non-stories about the decision, reactions and analyses, and lots of spin from both sides.

Clearly this was the end for Gore. Bush had stalled so long, warning that Gore was trying to steal the election, that he had managed to steal it himself. Despite the fact that more people had voted for Gore. The results made me grumpy.

We wandered through our Shinagawa neighborhood at the height of the dinner rush, looking for a restaurant. Several times I wanted to leave and hole up at the Pacific with room service. But I couldn't handle any more TV, especially rehashing that day's news.

We found a place and, for some reason, ordered horse sashimi. "Hmmm, nicely marbled," said Larry.

"Very cold," said Randy as he wolfed it down.

"I've been friends with too many horses to eat one," said Jon, a Texan.

Bush or not, we had to focus on our upcoming match. This was a big night: bowling for the budget of the film. We teased Randy.

How would he explain to Jane—his wife, partner, and executive producer of our project—that he had lost the budget in a bowling competition? They had co-produced this film and others for the company, and it would be bitter news and financial ruin if Randy and Jane were forced to do this complex international project for free ... but it was a joke, right?

The clients greeted us warmly at the Lanes as they stretched and loosened up. Without their ties and jackets, they looked less like timid bumblers and more like slim, agile, athletes. And they averaged about 15 years younger than our graying Team USA.

We may have been grizzled, but we were serious, and we stayed pretty even for the first couple of games. None of the clients had bowled for a while (except Takk, who went back to using his surname), so at first our recent experience gave us an edge. We led them by a total of 25 pins after the first game, and by 15 pins after the second. But by the third game, especially after working long hours that week, we were tired. The clients, refreshed from days of *watching* us work, gained strength (and pin count) as the evening wore on.

Larry had a pretty good evening and Jon held his own. Despite my earlier successes matching Randy's scores, I choked badly that night. The miracle hook on my ball went back into hiding. My strikes were scanty and my spares were sparse. But Randy was our star.

His right leg had been aching since the night we'd bowled five games with Takk. I had given him two Motrin tablets, to take four hours apart. He ignored my advice and took them both together (This reminded me of our trip to Africa years before, when he carelessly took six weekly doses of the malaria drug Lariam *at one time*). The Motrin relieved his pain for a while, but as the evening wore on, it began to wear off and I had no more.

Nevertheless, on this biggest of all bowling nights, he led our scoring. As I rolled open frame after open frame, he put up spares and strikes galore. Sometimes he limped a little, like a puppy with a bandage hoping for sympathy, but I could tell his leg was actually quite painful.

In our final game, Randy had a strike in the third frame, then another in the fourth, and another, and another. In the seventh, though, with the game and match on the line, his first ball left him with a 5-7 split.

He flung the second ball down the alley with his typical twisty-wrist action, adding some special body English on his follow-through as he landed hard on his right foot. The aching leg collapsed under him, and his tush whapped hard on the wooden lane. Ka-thud!

Yet his gyrations somehow convinced the ball to graze the 5 pin at an acute angle and slither it neatly across to topple the 7 in the far left corner. Split converted, spare made! Cheeks on the hardwood, he threw out his arms in a triumphant gesture.

We hauled him to his feet and applauded his display of athletic finesse. He finished that game with 178, the highest individual score of the evening.

Despite Randy's heroics, the three clients beat us badly enough in the third game to win the match. We had a great time, cheering each other's spares and strikes and bemoaning our splits and sevens, but they beat us fair and square. The company won the Showdown.

As we started down the hill that foggy night, the clients proposed that we go drink together, but we still had one more day of shooting, packing, and a long flight home. Getting sloshed wouldn't help. I hoped we weren't committing some cross-cultural faux pas by turning them down, but they good-naturedly and limply shook our hands, thanked us for the match with big smiles, and bade us each good night.

Larry and I stopped at Mario's for ice cream, but neither of our girl friends was there. We chatted with the other clerks, but they wanted to close, and it wasn't the same. As we walked through the neighborhood licking our gelato cones, a well-dressed woman appeared out of the crowds, and crooned to Larry, "You want sexy massage, Mister?" then to me, "You want sexy massage?" We declined and brushed past her, giggling as we entered the hotel to a chorus of "goodeveningsirs." But we knew we had lost our match, and our pride drooped as limply as the hanging chad in Florida, a sad reflection of what might have been.

I slipped out of the Pacific for my Egg McMuffin Set again the next morning, and a pretty, round-faced young woman in a wool coat and tartan plaid skirt accosted me on the street.

"Hello. Do you know me? Do you remember me?" she asked demurely as she searched my face for signs of recognition. She looked familiar, but it took me a minute to realize she was one of the girls from the gelato place. I had never seen her outside of Mario's or out of uniform. Somewhat formally, she asked how much longer I would be in Japan. I told her it was my last day. With a sad smile and a bow, she wished me a safe and pleasant journey. It was a melancholy exchange.

We completed our final interviews in a drab conference room at the company's ultra-modern office building in central Tokyo. After hours on the phone, despite the fact that it's hellishly difficult to get one-day rush service on bowling trophies in Japan, Carole magically produced huge, personalized loving cups for each of our client opponents. The brass plaques read *US-Japan Bowling Championships*, along with personal alliterative nicknames—*Killer Kobayashi, Shooter Shimada,* and *Assassin Asahi*. Randy solemnly presented these gaudy mementoes to our clients at the conclusion of filming, in a thrilling display of international sportsmanship.

They invited us out to a Victory Dinner at a basement restaurant nearby. The beer and scotch flowed freely. We bowed a lot and laughed and toasted each other and our bowling prowess. We got to meet the Boss of our clients, the man who had pulled the strings behind the scenes during our shoot in Tokyo. Mostly he sat smiling quietly at dinner, wreathed in cigarette smoke, as his underlings, our client bowling team, fawned over him.

One of the clients drank too much and spent the dinner staring morosely at his trophy, muttering repeatedly to Jon, "I've never won anything before. Never won anything."

He sat down next to Larry and wept, pouring out his heart: he worked too much, he hated his job at the company, and his young daughters loathed him because he was never home. Despite the presence of his colleagues and the structured formality of their professional relationship, he was frank about his frustrations in this after-work and alcohol-enhanced setting. Next day, by custom, his coworkers would forget what they had heard.

Another of our clients told me that his own wife and daughter had just come to Tokyo that week from another city, to live with him for the first time. Though he had been married for four years and a father for two, they had never lived together, which was not uncommon in Japan. I was touched and thanked him for sharing this. Clearly bowling boosted rapport. Though we were very different (and they were still indecisive bumblers), ultimately our concerns were the same: family, kids, work.

We finished dinner and hailed cabs. One client, the Weeper, hung on Larry and begged: "Take me to America with you!" Larry peeled him away carefully, we said a gentle goodnight, promised to come back and bowl with them again someday, and went to our hotel to pack.

Beset by neon visions of the Showdown at Shinagawa and trying to forget that night's election results at home, I dumped clothes into my suitcase.

Our weeks of bashing heads with the clients over logistics clattered around in my brain: *Can't we schedule that sooner? Later? Tomorrow? Are we shooting here or somewhere else? When? What's it like there? Why can't we scout it now? Why can't you make a decision?*

I think the clients cared more about winning than we did, for they treasured their victory—and their trophies. Bowling gave them a way to relax with us, a brief respite from the grindstone of work. In a funny way, I knew I'd miss them, like our gelato girls.

Few tourists go to Tokyo to bowl; I never saw other foreigners at Shinagawa Lanes. For us bowling was a bit of exercise, a relief from the tedium of making a corporate film in a resistant culture, a campy diversion from the political zoo in the U.S we watched from afar, a way to connect with others, and a sideways glimpse of modern Japan. Even though we lost the Showdown.

If only we'd taken Randy's advice and knocked down more pins.

Epilogue: After our return from Japan, Jon went back to Texas, but Randy and Larry and I bowled regularly at my home lanes in California for several years, eventually improving and buying our own shoes and balls. We still bowl together from time to time. Months after the Showdown, we bowled again with two of the same clients, who had come to San Francisco to review a later stage of the film we shot for them.

No betting this time, no weeping, and no regrets.

China

Shanghai Lunch

One of the perks of business travel is the opportunity to sample local cuisines, often expanding our appreciation of dishes that never make it to the States. Japan offers delectable gustatory treats, beyond the sushi-tempura-teriyaki triumvirate prevalent at home. Paris, of course, is the ultimate source of fine French cooking of all kinds, and a trip to Mexico opens a gringo's eyes to a broad range of *comidas mexicanas*. So on a recent filming trip to Shanghai, we looked forward to some good meals.

Four of us were traveling from the States with 13 cases of camera and audio equipment, the final leg of a long video shoot that had taken us through the U.S., Europe, and now China.

Our arrival was inauspicious. When we landed in Shanghai Tuesday evening, we learned that the Customs officials had just decided the cash bond to bring in our gear would be $11,000 US, not $7000, as they'd said earlier.

"Chinese people, and government, like to keep you off balance," said Andrew, our Chinese producer from Hong Kong. "Everything is simple, but complicated." So he and his assistants scurried around that evening, long after banks were closed, to find the extra cash, while Jim, our video engineer, stayed with the gear in the airport for several hours until the situation was resolved.

Next morning, Wednesday, the Important Doctor we had come to Shanghai to interview told us that he was unavailable either of the next two days (despite weeks of planning around that schedule) and we had to film his interview that same day. Problem: our lighting crew and equipment were booked only for Thursday and Friday, our scheduled shoot days. Wednesday, our first day on the ground, was supposed to have been our scouting and planning day.

The Important Doctor was immovable, and we left the hospital for a couple of hours of planning and R&R, discouraged and jetlagged. Stuck in the hospital's working-class district a long way from downtown, we consulted two of our clients from the giant medical company that had brought us to Shanghai to film the Important Doctor: where should we have lunch? They led us to a neighborhood restaurant.

It seemed like a nice place at first, lots of potted palms and spacious booths. But we were the only Western faces in there, and they immediately stuck us in a private back room with uncomfortable benches. Waiters dropped by every now and again to provide grudging service.

The menu had dozens of glossy pages with photos of food and drinks. Only twelve hours off the plane, we four gringos were thirsty and dehydrated. Since Andrew has always cautioned us against tap water or ice in China, we asked for bottled water. The waiter shrugged and shook his head.

"This really isn't a tourist place," said Andrew.

"Well, what do they have to drink?" I asked. "What do they serve?"

Long discussion with the waiter. "Beer. And soft drinks," said Andrew.

"Great," said Jim. "I'll have a Coke."

Another long discussion. No Coke. No Pepsi.

"Uh, what soft drinks do they have?"

"Look in menu."

Tea, of course, and lots of unusual concoctions with medicinal or floral names we'd never seen or heard before. Beer wouldn't mix well with our sleep deprivation. Our producer Lori ordered bubble tea, a cold sweet tea drink with an unusual ecru color. I blithely ordered something that sounded similar. When hers finally arrived, she realized it contained ice and never touched it. The waiter eventually brought us small glasses of very hot water, recently boiled, but it was a long time before these cooled enough to be drinkable. My "soft drink" concoction had ice and an alarming blue glow, so for most of the meal I surreptitiously sipped water from a bottle I had carried in my pocket since our flight from San Francisco.

All this was coupled with the discovery that the rest rooms at that restaurant had only urinals and straddle-crappers, the traditional porcelain-lined holes in the floor for squatters (with footprints). No Western toilets. For me, that was a low point. We were truly off balance.

And so it went. We assumed we would eat family style as we do at Chinese restaurants in the States, so we each ordered a dish to share. They came out as individual lunch plates with rice, rather than a la carte dishes, but we clumsily tried to share them anyway. Awkward! The restaurant had no other plates available to help us share. No other plates!

Stuck on the bench at the end of the table to accommodate my long legs, I had to stand up and lean across people to reach the food, using chopsticks to scoop small amounts of greasy chicken curry and rice from two bowls onto a napkin in my hand, then struggling to maneuver this catch into my open maw. About as graceful as a sea lion eating pilaf with his flippers. Most of the food was thickly breaded and deep fried, or tasteless and dried out. The service was indifferent. All in all, a difficult meal.

But during that lunch, Andrew revealed (for the first time!) that he'd had an inkling of the doctor's scheduling problems the day before, had rebooked our lighting equipment rental and local crew. And as we ate, he received confirmation that Dragon Lau, a lighting professional we'd worked with several times before, had hopped on an early morning train from Hong Kong and would arrive in Shanghai soon. So Andrew expected to be able to field a fully equipped lighting team by 2 p.m. Despite the lousy lunch, our luck was starting to turn.

"Wow, this might just work," breathed Randy.

"Should be okay," said Andrew.

We chuckled. "So, you're not saying it *will* be okay, just that it *should* be," said Randy, our director, teasing Andrew about his typical, qualified response to our constant questioning.

Andrew was as good as his word. By mid-afternoon Wednesday, Dragon and his local cohorts had joined us at the hospital. We soon lit and shot the interview with the Important Doctor and the next morning, Thursday, with his head nurse. Both described the non-invasive techniques of coronary angioplasty, where they used amazing (and fabulously expensive) imaging devices made by our clients to see blockages in the heart and blood vessels, and to open them up by inflating coronary balloons or inserting metal stents. They told us of an 80-year-old patient who lived in the neighborhood and was thriving after such a procedure, and promised to put us in touch with him.

So our second morning was more satisfying than our first. This despite the fact that the hospital, a bastion of modernity and health, also sported straddle-crappers, and they were none too clean. Certainly we deserved a fine lunch.

Andrew and his crew took us to a different restaurant with a huge lobby area, where many of the available dishes were on display. Lots of fish (both dead and alive), shrimp and shellfish (alive), turtles (dead), and a variety of mysterious Chinese dishes.

I've never been a big fan of the kill-to-order thing, where they plop a living critter into boiling water or a sauté pan to satisfy your lust for tender flesh. We weren't sure the fish looked fresh, Jim's had problems with shellfish before, and I really didn't want to eat turtle. We'd already been on the road for four weeks together and weren't feeling too adventurous. We all wanted something yummy but safe. I asked whether we were doing family style today, but no one wanted to commit. After the mediocre meal the day before, we were each feeling possessive.

Then Lori spotted something that seemed familiar. It looked like chicken, delicately fried to a golden brown with merry little chunks of red pepper, zesty diced green onions, and toasted, slivered almonds. "Is this like a Kung Pao chicken?" she asked.

"Kind of," said Andrew. "But not much meat." Puzzled by this, we nevertheless all dove in together. Four orders of the Kung Pao-like thing. Andrew looked bemused, but said, "Sure, should be okay," and engaged the waitress in a lengthy discussion while repeatedly flashing four fingers. We headed off to the dining room.

Again, we were the only Western faces. This time it was family style. Andrew and our Chinese crew had ordered several dishes spun gently on a large lazy Susan, but I've never been fond of eating shrimp with the head, eyes, shell, feet and feelers intact, especially ones I watched swimming around happily only a few minutes before. The four of us mostly waited for our golden-brown comfort food. The Kung Pao-like thing.

Our chicken dish arrived in a large serving bowl, and Andrew had the waiters divide it into four smaller portions. It smelled heavenly, and by now I was hungry, breakfast a dim memory. As I started to tuck into this treat, Lori said, "Oh, I've got a little bone here."

Jim said, "Me too, several bones."

Randy: "Mine's all bones."

Silly people. How bad could it be? I bit down. It smelled great, and the first tickling of my taste buds was high on the yum scale. But as my teeth sank into the meat and veggies, I encountered an unexpected texture, too soft to shatter my dental work, but too crunchy to grind up thoroughly. I chewed and sucked around the hard parts, unsure how to react. The red peppers were pretty hot. If I avoided them too, there wouldn't be much left to eat but a little onion and an occasional almond sliver.

Despite not wanting to offend our Chinese hosts, I couldn't get through even one bite without spitting. I grabbed a small plate and quietly expelled a gob of partially chewed chicken, which, alarmingly, differed little in appearance from the unchewed chicken. Though the pieces did look a bit smaller.

We all looked to Andrew for guidance. "What is this?" I said, mortified at my inability to masticate my food.

"I told you, not much meat," he said with a grin.

"But you didn't happen to mention it was all bone," said Randy.

"Not all bone," said Andrew. "It's a delicacy in northern China."

"What's it called?"

Andrew exchanged some words in Mandarin with Vincent, our Chinese translator, trying to find the right meaning. Vincent consulted the Chinese-English dictionary app on his iPhone.

"Here it is: *cartilage*."

"Cartilage?" we echoed. "We've been eating cartilage?"

"Yup, you ordered it," said Andrew. "Four orders." He couldn't help laughing.

"Andrew," said Randy, "this reminds me of the time in Taiwan when you let me order duck web soup, but *you* wouldn't touch it with a ten-foot pole."

"Yup, you want it, I order that for you too. But I never eat that stuff." For half a dozen shoots in China and Hong Kong, Andrew had been our local producer, our fixer, our man on the ground, and he'd order whatever we requested, with a chuckle.

The others had sucked all their bones by now or had lost their appetites, but I was still hungry, so I shared one of the other dishes the crew was sharing on the lazy Susan: congealed pork cubes. A bit gelatinous in texture, but delicious. Slimy, yet satisfying.

After our lunch of gristle and slime cubes, we walked over to the apartment of Mr. Wu, the Important Doctor's 80-year-old patient, who lived a few blocks from the hospital. On the way, Vincent, who looked like he might blow away in a stiff wind, questioned me about my musical preferences: "What is your favorite jazz?"

"I love Miles Davis and John Coltrane."

He looked puzzled. "Who are they?"

"Jazz musicians. Americans. What kind of jazz do *you* like?" I crossed the street just as the light turned red. He hung back timidly and called out, "I love you for sentimental reasons!" It took me a minute to realize that he was referring to a song by Nat King Cole.

Mr. Wu was a retired engineer, and his apartment consisted of a large living-dining room, a terrace, several bedrooms, a tiny kitchen, and a couple of bathrooms, on the tenth floor of a modern building. The ten folks on our crew filled the place up, along with four or five of Mr. Wu's family. Two of our clients arrived a few minutes later, a doctor came over from the hospital (though not the Important Doctor himself), and some neighbors dropped by to see what was happening.

The apartment began to resemble the Stateroom Scene from *A Night at the Opera*, the Marx Brothers' classic.

Everyone in the apartment watched with smiles as we gingerly moved bulky furniture and stumbled around them and ourselves trying to set up our camera, lights, and sound gear. Andrew sent two assistants out on errands, and other Wu friends came in, along with two additional lighting crewmembers. Each time we changed camera setups, the throngs in the apartment shifted seats and vantage points as Dragon Lau, our lighting gaffer from Hong Kong, barked orders at his local assistants.

Mr. Wu looked great on camera, a strong, handsome face with impossibly jet-black hair. We settled down to chat. The medical terminology proved difficult for Vincent (a recent graduate of translation school, who was so nervous he was shaking), especially with Wu's thick Shanghainese dialect, but we got through it with much help from Andrew.

Mr. Wu told us the story of his coronary procedure and the relief of his pain and other symptoms. Then he asked, "Why do I look so young? Because I don't worry too much and I stay positive." And, he said, he liked to sing.

On cue, his middle-aged son and teenage granddaughter arrived, and we filmed Wu and granddaughter sitting at the piano. He picked out a few notes on the keyboard and grunted through some vague vocalizations— hardly musical, really, but who was I to poo-poo his singing, if these atonal utterances kept him young? Granddaughter, who was quite tall, launched into the first dozen bars of "Humoresque," then dissolved in a fit of adolescent embarrassment.

Next morning, Friday, we arranged to film Mr. Wu walking down the street and shopping at a food market across town. It was great to see him fully recovered, active, and out in the world. We had fun joking with the food vendors and cajoling them into appearing on camera with him, alongside displays of fruit, vegetables, Chinese herbs, sides of beef, dead fish, and three-foot-long eels. Our shoot ended on a high note. We had a great story, our long road shooting this medical film across three continents was coming to an end, and … it was time for lunch.

This time, on our third attempt, we hit the lunch jackpot. Andrew took us to a magnificent dim sum place in the Golden Magnolia Plaza skyscraper, adjacent to the Buckingham Palace karaoke club. We spotted something on the menu called Spicy Jew's Ear, but we decided to gorge ourselves triumphantly on Shanghai steamed buns, chicken pot stickers, rice noodle rolls, tasty pork and taro dumplings. Family style, light and delicious. A variety of drinks. Fresh Oolong tea. Bottled water, no bubble tea. No Coke, only Pepsi.

I found out later that Spicy Jew's Ear was a type of mushroomy fungus, but it still didn't sound like something I wanted to try. We stuck with foods we knew and had a great feast. And best of all, no one served us cartilage.

Wrecks and Pissers:
The Bombay-Pune Road

The notorious Bombay-Pune Road snakes and twists from the Indian Ocean up to the Deccan plateau. Centuries ago, this ancient trade route linked the coast to the interior. Silk and spice caravans passed this way, trying to evade bandits lurking in the rocky hills of the Western Ghats, a stretch of mountains dotted with cave temples and fortresses. Around the turn of the century, it became the treacherous setting for our spontaneous travel game.

Officially, the Bombay-Pune Road was India's National Highway 4, a paved two-lane blacktop with impossible switchbacks, unbanked turns, and deadly drop-offs that made us pray for a guardrail. Traffic gushed and careened: cars, public buses and colorful lorries skidded around the turns, passing each other on the left and the right, honking constantly in the blaring staccato symphony of the Indian roads. Most lorries bore odd signs that said "Horn-OK-Please" and hand-painted images of Shiva,

Vishnu, Brahma, Ganesh or other deities that protected them in the endless game of Tandoori Chicken played against all other drivers.

I had heard of this stretch of highway long before coming to India. Years ago, my friend Roshani's mother had been involved in a collision with a lorry on the Bombay-Pune Road. The family driver was killed, and her mother and two sisters were all injured, one bedridden for life. Such calamities were typical. From 1996 to 2000, the Indian government estimated an average of over 4,100 accidents *per year* on this 170-kilometer stretch of NH4—3,300 of them head-ons.

We had landed in Bombay two days before, on our way to Pune for a week's filming on a project about technology's spread to the far reaches of the world. Pune (or Poona, as it was known under British colonial rule) had several technical universities and was home to many information technology companies.

Sushil, our local production manager, had impressed us with his thoughtful diligence in a series of flowery emails during the weeks leading up to our arrival. We were curious about why he had arranged for a full-size, 60-passenger charter bus to take us to Pune, despite the fact that there were under a dozen in our party. Randy, Larry, Jon, and I were the American film crew. The rest came from Sushil's company, which we had hired to help us on the subcontinent: his sidekick, Manju; production coordinators Om and Mangal; our chief lighting technician, Heera; and a production assistant we referred to as L.C., because he was a bit of a loose cannon, boisterously offering us beer every morning at 8 (his last job had been with a German crew), or providing scalding hot black coffee undrinkable in any climate, especially in hot, muggy India (and then discarding it when I set it down to cool). The rest of our lighting crew traveled separately.

The occupants of the bus also included the driver and his boy, a helper-apprentice present on every truck and bus in India. The boy helped the driver stow cargo and passengers, hopped out to guide the bus in and out of tight spots, washed windows, and ran for snacks and drinks.

On the way to Pune, the number of accidents at the side of NH4 alarmed and perplexed us. Many vehicles, mostly lorries, had smashed into rock walls, fallen into ravines, or flipped onto their backs like marooned turtles. Some were rusted-out hulks close to the side of the road. Others looked as if they might have skidded off the road moments before. Why were so many wrecks left in place? Didn't anyone want them? Were there still bodies in them? The disorientation of driving on the left side added to our edginess.

NH4 was scary enough, but the situation was complicated by the construction of the Mumbai-Pune Expressway on a roughly parallel route. Mumbai is the original city name for Bombay, the latter a vestige of British colonial rule. Though the city had recently been named Mumbai again, both names were still used in modern India.

Building of the Expressway had dragged on for five years. Environmentalists fighting it had estimated the construction would destroy 800 species of flora, 80 species of butterflies and the habitat of the Giant Malabar Squirrel. Eventually it would be a six-lane superhighway speeding commuters between the two cities. But on the day we drove to Pune, the Expressway was still a series of short bursts of new road set in the ancient hills, often separated from the old road by detours that led us bouncing over fields of gravel, rock, mud and dusty dirt.

Now we began to appreciate Sushil's wisdom in hiring such a leviathan vehicle. The sheer mass of our air-conditioned, padded-seat behemoth gave us a feeling of stability on the rocky terrain. Lorries cautiously backed down from risking a head-on with us. And the 60-seater provided a stable camera platform for grabbing shots of the countryside during the ride.

The terrain presented a smorgasbord of sights: lush, fertile valleys with palm trees; dry, scraggy, rocky, reddish-brown mountains; barefoot laborers in numerous construction areas, the men bare-chested with baggy white shorts, the women in brightly colored saris tucked up around their waists as they schlepped rocks or mixed mud bricks or carried ridiculous burdens on their heads. We saw families living on the streets or in fields near the road or in cardboard cartons or crude shacks made of tin sheets, bathing in culverts, drinking brown water that made us shudder. People of all ages and genders ate, drank, urinated, and defecated everywhere, without self-consciousness. Apprehensive about our surroundings, we tried to enjoy our smooth ride in hermetically sealed, refrigerated luxury. Suddenly and without warning, a trailing explosion of yellow vomit erupted from the rear window of a dusty, open-air public bus in front of us.

After nearly three hours of slithering up the old road and scrabbling back and forth to the new one, we stopped at Khandala, one of two lush hill stations midway between Bombay and Pune. The driver took a break, and we enjoyed a cool drink as our Indian friends told us about second-century Chaitya caves in nearby Karla, with ancient wall carvings and inscriptions that told tales two millennia old. We hopped back on the bus for another two hours watching the lorries, the traffic, the wrecked hulks, the scenery, and the poverty, then finally arrived in Pune, applauded the driver for his efforts, and dashed into the cool comfort of our hotel. It was beastly hot in the open air, and we hadn't been in India long enough yet to acclimate.

We spent a week in Pune, the major educational and technical center for Maharashtra State, conducting interviews, filming people on the street and colorful scenes of Indian life, and seeking out dot-com and high-tech signage and other imagery to illustrate our story. Earlier that month we had been filming in Costa Rica and Alaska for the same project. At that time, the term *blog* was not yet common parlance, but I had posted a daily journal and photos from those shoots on my website, and we were thrilled to discover that our Indian crew had read about our earlier exploits before we arrived in Mumbai.

Sushil and Manju and their team took great care of us. Can we shoot in an elementary school? Easy. A college? No problem. All accomplished with a sweet Indian calm we grew fond of. At breakfast one day, Sushil spotted a story in the newspaper about an 11-year-old boy recently named the youngest Microsoft Certified Professional in India. Did we wish to interview him? We were shooting in Prattik's home by 2.

Whenever we were shooting out on the street, curious passersby would stop whatever they were doing and watch us film buildings, vehicles, and crowds. Often under foot, they would sometimes come up to our camera and look through it, uninvited, or pose with us for pictures. Staring seemed to be the national pastime, never aggressive or threatening, but this lack of social boundaries could still be disconcerting.

One day, for example, we were shooting scenic vistas from an outdoor stairway at a Hindu temple high above Pune. With our Sony F-900 HD camera on a tripod, I was picking off shots of the boats, crowds, and traffic by the river far below us. I didn't realize that Larry and Randy had drifted off to explore the other side of the temple. When I took my eye off the viewfinder, my friends were gone, and I found myself surrounded by a half dozen local men, all watching me closely. I looked down. Jon sat on the ground near the tripod, with a black cloth over his head in the searing heat, tweaking the exposure and color of my shots, a 9" video monitor in his lap, a remote camera control unit in his hand. Smiles all around.

Many Indians share this curious disregard for quaint Western ideas of personal space. Each morning of our shoot, production assistant L.C. would show up in Jon's hotel room much too early, to help move the video gear down to the lobby. Some days he would burst in the door as Jon opened it, dash inside, and grab and tug at the equipment cart. If Jon wasn't ready to send it, he would wrestle L.C. for the cart and implore him to wait ... and L.C., the Loose Cannon, would hang around waiting and watching as Jon finished dressing.

"So I'm standing there in my towel," Jon said, "just a little self-conscious as I'm brushing my teeth, and he's standing about two feet away inspecting my toilet kit."

We drove around Pune in an air-conditioned van that played "Jingle Bells" as it backed up. Outside, the relentless onslaught of poverty depressed us. Hordes of poor people assailed us each day when we left the hotel grounds or walked around in downtown Pune. Dirty young mothers with pretty, Arian features and chestnut skin, some mutilated and missing hands or feet, would drag their babies to our car and rap repeatedly on the window, trying to get handouts as we waited for red lights.

At home on the streets of Berkeley I might give a quarter or more to a "spare change" guy. But pushy beggars made me squirmy, and I already felt guilty enough for being white, American, and middle class. Don't give them anything, our friends said. Donate money to relief agencies and charities, they told us—paying aggressive beggars only encouraged them to mutilate their children. But how could any relief agency or a hundred of them cope with the hundreds of millions of poor in India, people so poor they would damage their kids to make them more pitiful?

At the end of our week filming, our cynicism peaked as we boarded another whale-on-wheels and started back down the Bombay-Pune Road. Immediately we spotted a newly overturned car in a shallow ditch by a hairpin turn. As our air-conditioned tank crept past, we stared out the window at two men removing a fresh body covered with a blanket from the wreckage.

We glided away in silence. Soon this thoroughly chilling sight brought forth a common defensive response: irony. Jon suggested we keep an eye out for all totaled vehicles on the way back, even count them for fun. Across the road, a man relieved himself with his back to the traffic. Randy said he thought it would be more fulfilling to count people who were using the street as a toilet. And thus was born the game of Wrecks and Pissers.

It was a travel game similar to counting state license plates or finding consecutive letters in road signs, and the rules developed as we went along. Jon and Randy were the players, Larry served as judge and had to verify each sighting, and I was a self-appointed cheerleader, capable of supporting either side shamelessly. We awarded one point to Jon for each wreck he spotted and one to Randy for each pisser. Everyone felt that giving Randy both pissers and shitters would be too big an advantage.

Sushil and his gang observed us with wonderment. Manju laughed contagiously, and her glee kept the mood light. L.C. wasn't exactly sure what was happening, but he watched closely.

As time passed during the drive, we refined the game. Wrecks were defined as motor vehicles on their backs or sides or clearly unable to run because of impact with a tree, post, wall, rock, or, most commonly, another vehicle. Stalls didn't count, or the competition would be too unbalanced.

The beginning of the trip was primarily on the serpentine old road, and pissers abounded. At first, it seemed each player would score dozens of points, so we decided that 15 would win the game. Like racquetball.

We hadn't counted on the encroachment of modernity. It was soon obvious that the new road from Pune back to the coast was much more complete than it had been in the other direction. We drove mostly on the Mumbai-Pune Expressway, which had far fewer wrecks *or* pissers than the old road. It promised to be a low-scoring game after all.

In several hours, we reached the lowlands closer to Mumbai, and Randy led Jon by a slim 7 to 5. Scoring was infrequent, the light was fading, we were bored, and Heera filled the void by describing an interminable train trip with his family from Bombay to his home state of Uttar Pradesh in the north. Randy told Manju jokes to get her to laugh—fun, but no challenge. It began to rain lightly. As the sun sank below the horizon and emitted a reddish twilight glow, Randy saw a man urinating into a ditch at the side of the expressway. He roused Larry from a nap to get his sighting verified. A few minutes later, during a short stretch on the old road, Randy spotted another pisser: 9 to 5.

We passed a truck that had slid from the slick road into an embankment. The score was now 9-6, but Jon panicked as we detoured back onto the expressway. Since there were so few accidents and opportunities for him to score, he suggested a new rule: spotting an accident *in progress* would carry a bonus of five points. We all agreed, trying again to rebalance the game in a spirit of good sportsmanship.

Then Randy made his final score as we drove in awe past a man in a white turban, standing high atop a huge culvert pipe and pissing, quite literally, into the wind: 10 to 6. Grasping at straws now, Jon suggested an additional scoring possibility: If *our* vehicle was directly involved in a wreck, he would tally ten bonus points *and* an instant win. We laughed, discussed it at length, then agreed, as the remaining reflected sun faded slowly, leaving only a pale bluish skylight.

The rain picked up a bit, and we drove with the lights on. After 20 miles with no scoring, Larry suggested for the tenth time that we were probably done. Jon was tired of the stupid game and ready to throw in the towel. We'd been at it for hours, it was hard to see, and we were all cranky and tired of trying to be clever and witty.

"Let's call it off," Jon said.

I jumped in, the generic cheerleader-without-shame. "Hold on, Jonny," I pleaded. "There's still time left. The road's getting slicker with the rain, and maybe your luck will turn." Did I mention that it was easy to get cynical in India? The traffic slowed as we entered a construction area. An overturned car in a ditch added to Jon's wreck total, but another lorry standing at the side of the road appeared undamaged and was ruled a stall, and thus invalid. Randy now led 10 to 7, and Jon still wanted to quit.

We rolled into a rocky canyon and spotted a sign that read: "Danger. Accident Zone."

"See, Jonny?" I gasped. "It's a sign, I mean, an omen that you should hang in there." Heavy winds swirled around the steep rock walls and buffeted the bus. The road ahead was illuminated, and we watched transfixed as a colorful lorry about 50 feet in front of us slipped on a turn and skidded across the wet road. Our world segued sharply into perceptual slow motion. Complex, instant events seemed to drag out, and milliseconds felt like minutes. As the lorry driver braked sharply, his semi jackknifed, its cab twisted clockwise around the trailer, and it struck a four-foot retaining wall on the right side of the highway.

"Oh God," cried Randy. The rest of us were speechless, but no one missed the fact that Jon had scored a five-point bonus. To avoid the wreck in front of us, our driver jammed on the bus's brake pedal. With a loud "PSSSSSSSSHHHHT!" from the air brakes, we skidded on the wet pavement, and the left rear end of the bus fishtailed and smashed into the retaining wall.

We heard a disturbing crunching-scraping sound as we hit, but our impact was mild compared to our mass. No one in our motorcoach was hurt or badly shaken up. After deep breaths, we looked up the road. The driver of the wrecked lorry and his boy jumped out, unhurt, and lifted the hood, as a small cloud of steam wafted up from the engine. Cars streamed past them at high speed.

We all sat there for a moment, silently contemplating what might have happened. Then Jon jumped from his seat, threw his hands in the air in the touchdown sign, and yelled, "I won!"

An explosion of hollering consumed the bus—about the lorry, the game, the rain, the accidents, the traffic, the scoring. We all agreed that Jon's five-point bonus for witnessing an accident in progress had given him the lead. In any case, our own fender-bender gave Jon an instant win.

Months later, Jon told me that this time of triumph was "the moment when we all realized what assholes we were."

The game settled, we started to feel foolish. We trooped out of the bus and discovered, with a shudder, that we were on a bridge over a huge chasm. The low retaining wall we had hit was actually the side of the bridge, and the ravine below us fell away in the dark like a bottomless pit in Mordor. As Manju waited inside, the nine men in our party stood next to the bus and relieved themselves over the edge into the canyon. More than one of us calculated silently—not how close we had come to a calamity, but how nine pissers would have won the game for Randy, if not for the instant-win rule.

"You're never going to write about this," he growled to me.

40

"Never," I promised solemnly.

Traffic swooshed all around us. Our driver examined the side of the bus, which showed minor scrapes and dents. We shook his hand and laughed and congratulated him on avoiding injuries and minimizing damage. We got back on the bus—bored, tired, giddy, jet-lagged ... assholes.

As we pulled slowly away, we passed the wrecked lorry. The driver smiled sweetly at us and called out something with that odd Indian sideways shake of the head. The boy waved. A large painting of Ganesh, the god with the elephant head, watched over them from the side of the lorry. We drove on into Mumbai in silence. Game over.

China:
Globalization with a Vengeance

I sat by a window in a Starbucks on the outskirts of Hong Kong, in the border village of Lo Wu. It was the end of the railroad line, and I could see into China, as "Jingle Bells" played in the background.

The modern towers of Shenzhen loomed in the distance, but I couldn't go there. No visa. In the foreground, the Sham Chun River was lined with a tall wire fence, clearly designed to keep people *in* China, not out. Peter's parting tease to me a few minutes ago echoed through my mind, "Now you've got a great story! Most people are trying to *escape* Communist countries. But you're so lame you can't even sneak *into* China!"

Protestors were blocking the streets near the visa office. The irony was powerful enough to penetrate my jetlagged haze, for I represented the very globalization they abhorred.

I'd stumbled into this problem inadvertently. Ten days before, when I was in Shanghai on a film shoot, I received an email from Peter, a colleague in New York, telling me he had another, separate filming job coming up for me in Shenzhen. I'd never been to China before. Now, suddenly, I had two projects there in the same month. Because I had to leave Shanghai for a shoot in Mexico and a brief stopover at home in San Francisco, I needed another visa to return to China. Andrew, our Chinese producer, had assured me he could obtain it easily at the 24-hour visa office in Hong Kong upon my return.

Peter, on the other hand, wisely got his visa from the Chinese Consulate in New York before leaving. We had arranged to meet Andrew in Hong Kong, get my visa, then proceed across the border together into Shenzhen.

Even though the Brits handed Hong Kong over to China in 1997 after a 99-year lease, the Chinese have maintained the former colony—their golden goose and trading center for much of the world—as a Special Administrative Region, still using HK dollars, not Chinese Yuan. Visa required to enter China, but not for Hong Kong.

As I headed for the airport in San Francisco to return to China, an email from Andrew warned that riot police had cordoned off the street of the visa office on Hong Kong Island, to protect the conference of the World Trade Organization at the Convention Center next door. When I arrived the next day, Hong Kong's largest civil disturbance in twenty years rocked the streets around the WTO meeting. Seven thousand demonstrators had poured into town, including a feisty group of Korean rice farmers fighting globalization by opposing lower tariffs on the importation of rice into their country. They threw eggs and wielded long bamboo sticks menacingly as they battled 22,000 police in the streets.

Stuck without a visa, I rode the East Rail commuter train with Peter and Andrew from our Hong Kong hotel about 45 minutes to the Chinese border. In each coach, several large TV screens showed the latest news, accompanied by the cheerful strains of "Frosty the Snowman." We gawked at visuals of demonstrators with sticks, helmeted cops with clear plastic shields, blasts from fire hoses, clouds of tear gas, and the gull-winged Convention Center.

"See that pink building there?" Andrew chuckled. "That's the visa office! The pink one. There, see it again? Streets are closed for blocks around."

At Lo Wu, the end of the line, Andrew had hoped to arrange my visa at the border station, but it was closed. So Andrew and Peter walked across the pedestrian bridge into China, and on to the Shangri-La Hotel in Shenzhen. I waited in the last Hong Kong station at a Starbucks, next to a food stand called the Lost City of Snacks, for Andrew to return.

The Koreans were fighting globalization with violence. Their vehement resistance to the WTO worked. It was impeding my ability to do my job.

Much of my film work abroad has been for multinational high-tech and medical corporations in Europe, Asia, Latin America, and even Africa. I eat local food when I travel, avoid fast food and rarely drink the water, and my caffeine addiction helps me overcome the numbing jetlag.

As a San Francisco-based cinematographer working for a New York producer, flying separately on Singapore- and Hong Kong-based airlines, using Japanese-branded equipment to shoot a film in China interviewing the American general manager of a Japanese hard drive factory, I was an agent of the very forces the protestors opposed. Because of them, I was stuck at the border. And I was sitting in a Starbucks, the poster child for relentless global expansion.

The café was decked out for the holidays. "Hark the Herald Angels Sing" played as I looked out at Red China, waiting for Andrew to return. At my elbow, a card with the familiar green mermaid logo touted Gingerbread and Toffee Nut Lattes, in English and Chinese. Bilingual signs urged me to "Brew Up Some Starbucks Christmas Joy This Year" and reminded me that this seasonal hoo-hah "Only Happens Once a Year" and that "Cups Warm Hearts."

On the road, I often resort to Starbucks—drinkable, if not exactly fabulous, and usually better than the local swill. I've endured unspeakably, phenomenally bad coffee in Norway, Nagoya and North Dakota, and everywhere in between, and the mermaid can provide a welcome, reliable mediocrity in outlying areas. In the past two weeks, Starbucks baristas in Shanghai, Mexico City, Berkeley and Hong Kong have warmly wished me a Merry Christmas. Sometimes I explain that I am not a Christian, but they don't care, it's a commercial holiday. Globalization with a vengeance.

Eventually Andrew dropped Peter off in Shenzhen, picked me up at the station Starbucks, and we returned to my hotel in Hong Kong. The WTO meeting ended that night and the demonstrators disappeared.

Next day, Andrew waited for hours in a long line in Hong Kong to procure my visa, then we finally headed for the border in a hired car. After an uneventful crossing through what looked like a toll booth, our driver Simon pulled over, replaced his Hong Kong license plate with one from China, and moved from the left side of the road (a vestige of HK's British heritage) to the right side, conforming to traffic in China. He told me he crossed the border three or four times a day, sometimes more.

Our goal was to meet Peter at his client's new factory in Longgang on the other side of Shenzhen, but the area had grown eightfold in the past 30 years, and bad directions, dated maps, and poorly marked (or unmarked) streets delayed us for hours. I feared we were even beyond the reach of Starbucks. Eventually Simon hired a local motorcycle rider to lead us to the new industrial park. We found our destination as the winter sun set behind us.

At the factory gate, a pair of young private security guards in new, military-style uniforms blocked our way, red epaulets and gold shoulder braid jiggling as they argued with us. Despite the fact that Andrew had been on the phone all day with our clients inside the new factory, apprising them of our painfully slow progress, by the time we got there, our contact had left for the day. The guards maintained that they "were not informed" of our arrival and would not let us pass. The factory complex had just opened that day, and they didn't know how to call inside. In the waning twilight, we could see Peter through the glass walls of the building, impatiently pacing back and forth, unaware of our plight. He'd been waiting for us since 9 a.m. We yelled, jumped up and down, and waved our arms to attract his attention, but to no avail.

I implored the guards, with Andrew translating, to walk into the building and talk to the tall, burly, bald Caucasian, but they resisted. The plant was brand new, and they were not about to buck procedure, even if they weren't sure what it was. We soon made ourselves so obnoxious muttering menacing scatological incantations that finally one of them turned on his heel and sauntered slowly toward the entrance. Eventually we saw him inside talking with Peter and a young Chinese woman, and a flurry of activity ensued. The guards averted their eyes as they opened the gate, and I shouted something crudely Anglo-Saxon as we drove through.

Finally inside, I knew we had come to Longgang to work, to scout a location for our interview with the manager of the factory ... but I was beat. The long plane ride, the visa problem, the drive, the tension, the poor directions, our tardiness, and the recalcitrant guards, had all combined to sap my energy.

I knew what would hit the spot and help me reach my Target Heart Rate quickly: sucking down a Gingerbread Latte. Or Toffee Nut. Maybe cups do, indeed, warm hearts. But there wasn't a Starbucks in sight.

Globalization does have its limits.

New Zealand:
Living a Lie at Mrs. O'Brien's

Randy strode into the rundown house, took a quick look around, thanked the people who lived there, and hurried out.

"It just won't work," he sighed to Brent and me. "I wanted a location that could pass for a grandmother's house, but this looks like something from *Tobacco Road*."

We had a problem. Gerald and the rest of our lighting crew had already arrived, and we expected the Footes in an hour. If this house proved unsuitable, where would we film their interview?

Our story centered on a kindly old couple. Weeks before, when their car had broken down, Mr. and Mrs. Foote had called New Zealand Telecom's new 0-800 emergency road service number from their cell phone. We would reenact the rescue, happy to support this new service that was plucking stranded elderly drivers and their cars from roadsides across the island nation.

Randy, Jane, Rod and I were a small American crew, making a film for a Japanese manufacturer of telephone switching equipment. We had hired Brent as our local production manager, Gerald as our lighting gaffer, and several other Kiwis to fill out our crew.

Since this story was only part of what we needed to shoot in our few days in New Zealand and the chosen couple lived many hours away, we had decided to find a house closer to our base in Wellington for their interview.

"As long as we don't mind living a lie," said Randy. We didn't. We often filmed people in rented or borrowed locations.

So Brent had dispatched a production assistant to search for a suitable house in a small town an hour north of Wellington, but Randy had now nixed his selection. What to do?

"What kind of house would you like?" Brent asked him calmly.

"Something that looks like Grandma's house. That place was just too seedy!"

"Get in, and let's drive around."

"But you can't just pick a house at random and arrange it on the spot," Randy spluttered. For a moment, he looked worried.

"Get in."

We cruised with Brent for ten minutes, and Randy dubiously chose a house a few blocks away, a charming brick ranch with a "For Sale" sign and a huge palm tree out front. Mrs. O'Brien answered Brent's knock, and he explained our predicament. Recently widowed, she was happy to help, especially when she learned that Americans were involved and we would only need her dining room for a few hours. Of course Jane offered to pay her, but she refused.

"Ridiculous," Randy said. "In the States, no one would do this without references, location releases, permits or fees. You can't just bang on someone's door, walk in, and make a film." But Mrs. O'Brien, who really was a grandmother, welcomed us and served us cookies. Brent was not surprised.

We had encountered New Zealanders' inclination to be helpful the previous day, when we dropped by the Central Station in Wellington unannounced, to grab shots of commuters and trains during the morning rush. Rod and I set up my Arri 16SR camera and tripod hurriedly amidst a crowd of passengers, but we were too late to catch much of the next arrival.

A tall, mustachioed man accosted us. "Here now, what's this?" he barked, like a poor man's John Cleese in a stationmaster's uniform. Uh oh, I thought, busted. We had no permit or permission to shoot there. Brent explained chattily that his clients from America were in town to shoot a film for a big corporation.

"Oh, really?" said the stationmaster sternly, as he looked us up and down. I suddenly wondered if there were holes in my blue jeans.

"Yes sir," said Brent, "But they've missed the shot of the previous train pulling in. Can you tell us which track the 9:03 will arrive on, please?"

"Well," said the mustache, thoughtfully, "which track would you *like* it to arrive on?"

Rod and I looked at each other. "Track 12, please, sir," I piped up. "We can pan our camera over and get a clear view of the train pulling in, with the city in the background."

"Done." *Accommodating folk, these Kiwis.*

We interviewed a Telecom employee named Faye about the emergency road service. She happened to be an Olympic archer, so Randy also wanted a few shots of her plunking arrows into her practice target, a large, heavy, compacted straw affair called a butt. Because there were no obvious archery locations in downtown Wellington, we opted to haul Faye's big butt up two flights of stairs to the empty office where we filmed her interview. For one shot, I set the camera right next to the target and bailed out as she zipped several arrows close to the lens, each perfectly centered in the bullseye.

"Splitting arrows isn't actually that difficult," said Faye.

Wellington reminded us of San Francisco: a windy, hilly city on a beautiful bay, the Cook Strait between the North and South Islands. But New Zealanders' accents and idioms constantly reminded us we were not in California. On our first evening we went to dinner at a restaurant called Shed 5, which the locals pronounced Sheed, to rhyme with steed, not bed. The next day at dusk, we shot a red and fiery sun approaching tangency with a silky-calm, deep-blue ocean. Brent described the scene as beautiful but "a bit chocolate-boxy," which we took to mean lovely, but in a clichéd way.

Another time I told Brent I would meet him on the street as soon as I grabbed my fanny pack (a portable storage-and-transport case I wore around my waist), and I heard the Kiwis gasp and snicker. *What had I said?*

Finally he turned to me with a giggle. "Fanny, in N.Z.," (which he pronounced "En Zed), "refers to *women's genitalia*, not a derriere." Or a butt, apparently. They also tittered over the name Randy, so I often addressed him as Randall or Mr. Field. Or just Horny.

On a trip to the countryside outside the capital, we filmed sheep in fields, sheep by the side of the road, sheep closeups, and sheep in distant meadows against snow-capped mountains. This verdant nation, after all, was 50% pastureland: four million people and forty million sheep.

Back at Mrs. O'Brien's, we continued living a lie. We created a homey scene, arranging teapots and doilies and photos of the O'Brien children and grandchildren in the background of our interview shot with the Footes (the Feete?). Gerald and the lighting crew placed two HMI lights outside the window to imitate the sun, and streaked them into the dining room in a saucy way. The effect was convincing. The shot looked great.

"Oh, Gerald, I love how that looks!" I called out.

"Oh, gettin' a bit of a stiffy, are ya?" he responded with a smirk. At least I wasn't grabbing my fanny pack.

Mr. and Mrs. Foote proved amiable but soft-spoken, and their interview was challenging for Randy. At one point the light and shadow patterns coming through the window started to bounce around, and I called to Gerald and his lads to keep steady on the lights.

"Righty-o!" they called back. Soon it happened again.

"We're having some difficulty with the wind and the rain," yelled Gerald. I was puzzled. From inside, my view out was partially blocked, but our phony interior sunshine made it seem like a beautiful day. I went out to the side yard to see what was happening.

A remarkable scene greeted me: sunny, rainy, and windy, all at once. It was springtime south of the Equator, and the sun was climbing high in the clear, blue October sky. At the same time, a stiff breeze from the ocean was shaking our lights and blowing rain *sideways* past the house from a storm miles away.

Just then, the cops dropped by.

"Your neighbor reported seeing some lads loading a van in front of the house," the constable told Mrs. O'Brien. "Just wanted to make certain they weren't burglars." Mrs. O. introduced us like old friends and assured them of our good intentions. At that point she'd known us about two hours. Eventually we completed the interview and finished the cookies.

"Brent, that was a delightful scene," I said as we took our leave of Mrs. O'Brien.

"Oh it's just a bunch of fluffy ducks, isn't it?" he responded. I recognized those as English words, but the meaning escaped me. Clearly he was speaking a foreign tongue. Something was fluffy ducks, he explained, if it was just too cute for words.

We broke for lunch and planned our scene of the Auto Club assisting the Footes. We had selected a local country road for the reenactment.

It was then that they admitted the rescue story was bogus. The Footes had indeed been the recipients of roadside assistance, but they had called the Auto Club office directly, *not* through the new Telecom rescue number. The Telecom rep confirmed the new story a bit sheepishly, but without missing a beat, explaining that their new 0-800 number had just gone into effect in the past few days, long after they had recruited the Footes to be in the commercial. Had the new service been established earlier, our white-haired couple, of course, *would* happily have taken advantage of it. Our clients enthusiastically endorsed this feeble rationalization as sound reasoning.

"It *could* have happened that way," one muttered.

We were really living a lie now. But did it matter? We weren't promoting anything heinous, like war, murder, or cigarettes as a health food. Wasn't our scene still valid as a dramatization, of what could have or would have or should have happened? And besides—wink, wink, nudge, nudge— who would ever know?

After filming an interview with the Footes in bogus sunlight, in front of someone else's grandchildren and mementoes, we shot their car being towed by a wrecker they had never seen, with a driver they had never met, on a road they had never traveled, to promote an emergency phone service they had never used.

Then we headed back to Wellington. Mission accomplished.

21st-Century Village:
Telemedicine in Rural India

Outside, the temperature hovers near 100 degrees, the air still and the ground sere. A smear of recently graded, red-clay road trails through the dun landscape of the tiny Indian village of Thirukolakudi, as if spread there with a huge trowel by a giant. Our trucks and vans cluster near a small house by the side of the road, the only vehicles in sight.

Inside, I am sitting on the floor, a Sony F-900 HD camera cradled in my lap. I'm taking a shot of a telemedicine interface box, which accepts inputs from blood pressure, temperature, electrocardiogram, and pulse monitors, and displays them on the screen of a small computer. A 75-year-old man with white hair, bare-chested and wearing a white *lungi*—the traditional wraparound male skirt in southern India—sits on a cot, watching the process. He hobbled in earlier, complaining of a bad ankle and chest pains. A window on the computer screen shows the face of the man, and another displays live video of his doctor, a bumpy hour's drive away in Tirupattur, a small city of about 60,000. They converse in Tamil, the local language, and discuss the patient's symptoms and his vital signs on screen. Soon the doctor makes a diagnosis and prescribes medication.

I should feel cooler than I do, lurking close to the concrete floor. But as I look up from my camera, I realize one end of the small room is stuffed with villagers looking on. The inevitable Indian peanut gallery has gathered, and the heat of their collective curiosity adds to the suffocating atmosphere.

The operator of this Internet "kiosk"—really a small, narrow room in the front of the house—is a pretty young woman named Bharathi Sala in a blue sari and white scarf. She hooks EKG leads up to the patient's chest and attaches other cables to the telemedicine box, and she doesn't understand why we ask her to repeat actions for the camera. She rarely smiles.

As I grovel on the floor, our director Randy stands above me and attempts to control the situation. Communication is difficult. Sushil, our production manager from Bombay, doesn't speak Tamil, and the young local man we've hired to help with coordination and translation, strangely, is missing from the room. To fill the time, I photograph the faces of some of the villagers. They are unselfconscious, as interested in watching me work as I am in taking their pictures.

We've come to India to document a pilot government program to place similar kiosks in a few hundred villages. The operators are entrepreneurs trained for about a week in computer skills. They offer a variety of services to their communities—access to government records, English lessons, Internet tutorials, and, in some cases, medical consultations like this one. Bharathi, who comes from a neighboring hamlet, has had a few additional hours of medical training, and her kiosk has the extra diagnostic equipment necessary for telemedicine hookups. Eventually the Indian government would like to expand the kiosk program to more than 90,000 villages.

Our first shoot a few days ago was a story about local rice and sugar cane farmers obtaining tenancy and land ownership documents at an e-government kiosk in Sathnur village, near Bangalore in Karnataka State. Situated on a busy road with trucks, buses, motorbikes, and farm carts rumbling by outside, that kiosk had four computers, a printer, and the latest WiMax wireless broadband technology to connect with the Net.

Now we're in Tamil Nadu, the southernmost state in India, and Thirukolakudi makes Sathnur look like Manhattan. This village is electrified, like much of rural India, but few houses display more than a single standard fluorescent tube high up on the wall in each room. Outside Bharathi's kiosk, which has the same WiMax connection but only one computer, few people stir on the street and only an occasional bus rattles by. No private cars anywhere. Our bright blue generator truck looks out of place and time.

I have visited many countries with Randy and our producer Larry, but we've never strayed so far off the beaten path. On a previous trip to India five years earlier, we worked with Sushil in Bombay and Pune in western India, and endured the onslaught of beggars and street hustlers everywhere. But here in the south, traipsing through tiny towns where tourists rarely tread, we encounter calm starers who demand nothing and find us as exotic and studiable as we do them. We see no other Westerners for days at a time, other than a handful at our hotel in Madurai.

On the west side of Thirukolakudi, the severe drought which has plagued Tamil Nadu for the past couple of years chokes a large freshwater pond lined with lily pads and mud. Cows, goats and mangy dogs loiter around a few grassy patches, and three women are finishing their laundry on the opposite side. Looming over the pond, an unusual, bouldery rock formation thrusts upward, a Hindu temple chiseled high up into its core in a commanding view of the village. It's eerily quiet.

This village is small, no more than a few hundred people, with substantial houses and occasional thatched porches or outbuildings. Many of the men work in quarries in the area, and we see massive rocks along the roads and hear occasional loud stone crashes from the edge of the village.

Bharathi, now wearing a dark blue sari and bright pink scarf, poses for us outside her kiosk with her family, then her father proudly displays the degree she received for her computer studies. He introduces us to two teachers from the small schoolhouse down the street. While we've been shooting in the kiosk, Larry and Sushil have met with village leaders, made donations, and arranged for us to film at the school and at the temple on the hill. We always want to shoot portraits, show faces and environments, and establish the locale as a vital part of the story, so we're eager to see more of the village.

Randy and I take a break in the shade outside with Sushil and Larry, as our camera assistant Vinni changes lenses and our gaffer Kamlesh and the lighting crew set up to shoot in the school. The teachers, wearing elegant pale green and blue patterned saris, send the children out with plates of Sunfeast Glucose Biscuits, which we'd seen advertised in ubiquitous red-and-orange roadside signs. A whole plate for each of us. The kids range about six to nine years old. They giggle on back to the school and soon return with big smiles and tall glasses of cold water, which we turn down with polite regret—I can practically see the local microbes swimming around, grinning up at me as they plan havoc for my sensitive Western stomach.

To our amusement, Larry takes it upon himself to lead the children in a counting and clapping game, punctuated by much pointing and waving of arms. He loves kids and misses his three-year-old twin girls at home. We're fascinated to watch this, as the children mimic every word and gesture. In a finale to the game, Larry, a loyal San Francisco 49ers football fan, thrusts both hands upward and yells "Touchdown! Go Niners!" The kids reach for the sky, clueless about touchdowns but enthralled by the action.

When all is ready, the students sit on the floor of the school, and I wade on my knees amongst them, the video camera on my shoulder. The younger teacher leads them in a singsong English lesson, chanting "Roses are red, violets are blue..." They perform for her and for the camera with spirit and gusto. To support the words, the other teacher points to pictures of flowers and colors on the turquoise walls of the schoolroom, though they have trouble finding a visual for "sugar is sweet..." Clearly they are proud of their tiny school.

I watch the vivacious faces and sparkling dark eyes around me and wonder what will happen to these youngsters. I know many Indian people from the villages migrate to urban centers; will these students live their lives here, or will some opt to move away? Don't small-town kids everywhere long to leave for the big city, a frequent theme of literature and cinema? Will this one-and-a-half-room schoolhouse suffice for these kids? How many will move on to other schools?

Life has been flashing by me lately, and I'm trying to put it all into perspective. I first heard rumors of this trip to India only two weeks ago, which left just one hectic week of arranging crews, equipment, and logistics before our departure. Since landing, we've driven and flown over a thousand miles around India, and tomorrow we'll fly back to Chennai, for our fifth hotel in eight nights, then home to San Francisco. A whirlwind, to be sure, and I'm trying to gain some insight into what I'm seeing.

Working here with Bharathi and these dedicated teachers reminds me that some villagers seek education in order to offer services to their home areas. Not everyone wants to leave.

And meeting Dr. C. Sukumar, the physician on the computer screen who treated the old man in Bharathi's kiosk, is an uplifting experience. The doctor tells us he works with several such telemedicine kiosks and never charges for these remote consultations. He appreciates that the system saves many patients from having to travel long distances to see him, often on the bus with assisting relatives. It can take several people a day or more of travel and waiting to consult a doctor for one patient's complaints. Though he comes from another community about 120 miles away, Dr.

Sukumar settled in Tirupattur after his army service and medical training. He has also studied acupuncture and other alternative practices such as pranic healing, hypnotherapy, alpha mind power, and kundalini yoga, in order to broaden the range of treatments he can offer his patients.

"I still feel I have a long way to go in serving this community, notorious for superstitious beliefs," he tells us, "and most of my people here are illiterate. My social dream is to impart health education, screening, and free drugs for poor people. Telemedicine is an effective tool, but still a lot of motivation, cooperation, dedication, and training are required from the kiosk operator."

We are invited into a home near the kiosk to shoot portraits of a mother and daughter in their kitchen, cold tap and wood stove behind them. It's a rare and honored moment for us to be in someone's home while shooting abroad, and we appreciate the hospitality.

Barefoot at dusk, we slowly climb well-worn red-and-white stone steps to reach the 1500-year-old temple in the rocks above the village. Whitewashed walls and colored patterns line the lower stairwells and hallways. As I move higher, I look out pensively from porches and landings. Pastel-colored shrines, statues of Hindu gods, and inscriptions carved into natural stone walls cater a visual feast for our camera. I ask Sushil how many gods Hindus worship. "Thousands," he says.

"And how many temples are there?"

"Many thousands," he chuckles.

At the top of the temple, one of the minions rings a large bell with a chain clapper for us, a deep rich clang resounding across the village below. In a corner stands an odd blue-and-yellow contraption, a bell-cymbal-drum machine used for rhythmic clamor at significant rituals.

I lean on the railing after making my final shots of Thirukolakudi and ponder what Dr. Sukumar has told us. Though owner-operators like Bharathi must charge a few rupees for the telemedicine sessions (and currently a dollar buys over 40 rupees), the doctor proudly showed us a ledger book noting hundreds of patients he had treated for free, and many others for a song. Once he performed an appendectomy for 15 rupees.

I had a lively, one-sided discussion in Tamil this morning with the old man in the *lungi* who sought medical advice at Bharathi's kiosk. His prescription will be shipped by bus and arrive in a day or two. I understood not a word of language but easily grasped the severity of the pains in his ankle and chest. He was grateful to speak with the doctor from so near his own home and thanked us profusely, as if we had initiated the treatment, rather than simply recorded it.

Not everyone wants to leave for the big city, I think as I gaze out over the village, the red smear of road cutting through the landscape, and the odd, massive boulders strewn carelessly below us in the spreading shadows. Dr. Sukumar hailed from a different part of Tamil Nadu, then came to Tirupattur to practice. The telemedicine hookup expands his reach and his ability to deliver health care. I recall the teachers' pride in their school and the beaming smile of Bharathi's father as he showed off her accomplishments.

Some prefer to stay and serve.

See the film we shot in the Indian village at showdownatshinagawa.com

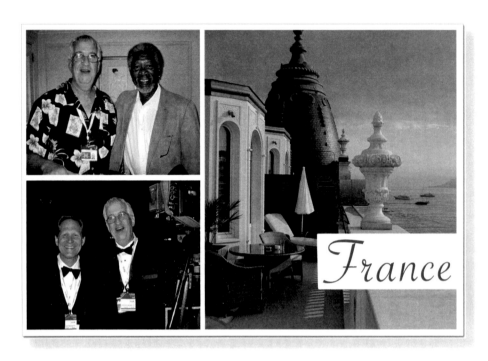

France

Starstruck at Cannes:
Morgan Freeman on the Red Carpet

"Two tips for the Cannes Film Festival," counseled a friend who had been there.

"First, pack your tux, because evening screenings are strictly formal for audiences and camera crews. A black suit and bow tie might pass, but a tuxedo is a better bet. Second, pronounce the name of the city the way the French do—*can*, as in beer can. Only the Brits say *con*."

"Whoa!" I splutter excitedly to Mark as we set up on the camera platform. In front of us, the Red Carpet swoops up the stairs to the Grand Theatre Lumiere at the Palais du Festival in Cannes. "There's Jackie Chan!"

I power up our camera, whip it around, and quickly roll some footage of the wildly popular Chinese action star as he poses with several other actors.

My family loves Jackie Chan, so I grab my little still camera, to snap souvenir shots for my wife and kids. Immediately, a manicured finger taps my tuxedoed shoulder. "I'm so sorry, but you're not permitted to take photographs from the television platform," explains our press contact Marjorie, a sweet young Parisienne who works at the Festival for a few weeks each year.

Mark and I have come to Cannes to film a project for an American computer chip company partnering with Revelations Entertainment— actor Morgan Freeman's production company—on the future of digital home entertainment. Morgan and Hilary Swank, both Oscar winners for *Million Dollar Baby*, are in town to present the *Palme d'Or*, the grand prize of the festival. Because Morgan and our other clients are attending tonight's premiere of *Sin City* at the Palais (known to locals as "le bunker" because of its blocky architecture), we are able to obtain this coveted spot just a few feet from *le tapis rouge*, the Red Carpet.

Two tiers of media occupy the platforms on both sides of the Red Carpet. On our upper level, TV cameras are wedged in, tripod-to-tripod, shooting every format from high def to DV. Our French crewmembers (who do indeed pronounce the city "can") have warned us that filming on the Red Carpet with our Sony F-900 camera could be a wild scene, with camera jockeys elbowing and crowding for better angles, but the other TV crews turn out to be quite civilized. In order to see over the photographers on the shorter platform in front of us, most video camera tripods are extended to full height, cameras raised above eye level, viewfinders pointed down, the operators forced to look straight up as they pan, tilt, focus, and zoom to follow the action.

On the platform below us, however, the situation is quite different. Here a pack of snarling mongrels in dress suits, equipped with expensive digital cameras and flash units, push and shove for position at the railing, holler to attract the attention of the passing stars, and scream with derision if the actors pass them by without posing. Hard-driving rock music played at earsplitting volume adds to this paparazzi chaos, along with enthusiastic but unintelligible announcements from an overdriven PA.

Jackie Chan wears a long black Chinese robe and is accompanied by the co-stars of his latest movie, *The Myth*. One in particular, a stunning brunette, stands arm-in-arm with him, then leaves the group and poses on her own for the photo dogs. Attired in a revealing white ensemble, with deep cleavage, bare midriff, and slit skirt, she stands saucily with her hand on one hip, blows kisses to the crowd, and patiently obliges the camera hounds on both sides. Yet the curs are never satisfied, barking "Turn left," "Over here," and "Turn right," and shrieking angrily—"No, no, where are you going?"—as she finally moves away. Wow, I think, who is that?

Cheering crowds applaud more stars and filmmakers as they are discharged from official Festival limos and repeat the same routine up the carpet. The flashes are nearly continuous and surely blinding to the subjects. The display of female flesh is remarkable. Is revealing clothing part of the dress code? Most women attending the screening, whether actors, jetsetters, tourists, or producers' wives, wear gowns with scoops or slits or openings in unusual places. What if women had to wear formal suits and men showed slews of skin, I wonder? Swedish supermodel Victoria Silvstedt appears in a black outfit that redefines low-cut and reveals parts of the derriere one rarely sees at public events. Healthy looking gal! Salma Hayek and *Spanglish* star Paz Vega glam their way up the rug.

Sin City directors Frank Miller and Robert Rodriguez arrive with most of the cast of their movie, many of whom we filmed the day before at a Miramax luncheon. Tonight's their premiere. Jessica Alba and Brittany Murphy wear elegant black gowns, surprisingly unrevealing, but the men take liberties with the sartorial rules. Though they all wear black suits or tuxedos, Michael Madsen sports a loose green tie, Mickey Rourke an open shirt, a string tie with a five-pointed star, and white boots, Rodriguez a bolo tie and, typically, a cowboy hat. Clive Owen and the rest eschew bowties for traditional long black four-in-hands. Benicio Del Toro chews gum and looks particularly ill at ease in the limelight.

Mark and I are scheduled to interview Morgan Freeman and his partners the next day for our film. Earlier in the week we filmed Morgan talking with critic Roger Ebert, as well as flavor shots of Cannes and the festival. But tonight our principal assignment is to document Morgan and our clients from the chip company, walking up the Red Carpet together.

Morgan's arrival is announced over the PA and cheered loudly during a rare break in the music. As they walk the Carpet, Morgan poses and pauses, scanning the camera platforms to find us among the tuxes and tripods. Mark calls out and waves, but the scene is loud and cameras are flashing as the dogs do their work. Finally he catches Morgan's eye after the group has passed us. Ever the showman, Morgan dances a graceful sliding two-step down half a dozen stairs toward us, finishing with a flourish and bow in front of our platform. With a wink, a wave and a thumbs-up, knowing we've gotten our shot, he rejoins his group, swings them in our direction for another quick wave, and then continues up the carpeted stairs to the Palais.

At the last minute, Liza Minnelli makes a dramatic entrance in a demure black shawl. Soon everyone attending *Sin City* has passed, and the crowds and media quickly disperse. The whole event is over in less than an hour.

But who was the brunette in white with Jackie Chan, I wonder? After we wrap, the Internet Movie Database reveals the names of his co-stars, including Bollywood actress Mallika Sherawat. I google her and find numerous news stories from the previous two weeks, breathlessly anticipating her arrival in Cannes with nearly a million dollars in jewelry.

Her appearance tonight quickly makes a splash back home. Catty designers, quoted in the *Times of India* only a few hours after she walked the Red Carpet, praise and criticize Mallika's ensemble. "It would have been better if there had only been one revealing element in the outfit—either the neckline or the legs," says Puja Nayyar.

"Plunging necklines are in, and the deep-cut choli looks sexy, but there should have been just a hint of the legs showing. The choli could have been worn with a voluminous skirt or jodhpuris with 2-3 belts at the waist to accentuate the lower half of her body, which is sexy." Shoulda, coulda, woulda.

Varun Bahl didn't like it either. "At a prestigious film festival like Cannes, Mallika could have dressed more stylishly. What she is wearing is not fashionable, it's like fusion wear. There are better ways of dressing up to look Indian." Ouch!

And designer Ranna Gill notes, "This particular ensemble is extremely oomphy, but that's Mallika for you."

I follow a link to an album of photos at Bollywood Sargam, a popular movie site with pictures of Jackie and Mallika from the Red Carpet a short time before. I want to see what the fuss is all about, to serve as an eyewitness to controversy, to assess for myself whether her choli should have had jodphuris. What is a choli, anyway?

In one pose, she and Jackie beam at the camera. In another, she blows a kiss to the snarling dogs. In a third, she smiles broadly, hand on hip. As I examine this last photo, I notice in the background, in the upper left corner of the photo, a bespectacled, tuxedoed, grey-haired man (once described by a friend as "tall, but Jewish") smiling broadly as he looks upward and away from Mallika. I know for sure he is staring up out of the photo frame into the eyepiece of a Sony 900, mounted high on a tripod, its viewfinder pointing down. And I'm certain that he's savoring the moment, happy to be there, feeling extremely oomphy.

It's me.

Tokyo:
The Tale of the 33rd Floor

Que sera, sera,

Whatever will be, will be...

Noburu had always been a Doris Day fan. He turned up the volume as he drove us toward Tokyo from Narita, the international airport. It was a long ride.

We had worked with Noburu twice before and he recognized me when we got off the plane. He was tall for a Japanese man, with a good sense of humor, crooked teeth, and a ready smile. He drove mostly for visiting film crews.

I loved Japan. As we approached the city, first passing Tokyo Disneyland and then a huge indoor ski jump, my excitement began to mount.

The future's not ours to see,

66

Que sera, sera.

On this trip in late November, Tokyo was flooded with Santas, candy canes, wreaths, drummer boys, nutcrackers, reindeer, and sleighs, and even an occasional nativity scene. The lobby of our hotel, the Pacific Meridien, held at least nine fully decorated Christmas trees.

Our rooms featured self-warming combination toilet-bidets found only in Japan. When I sat down, I heard warm water gurgling merrily to heat the seat from the inside. Press the wrong button (all instructions in Japanese) and Old Faithful gushed vertically. My pals insisted the hygiene and the eruption sensation were worth checking out ("I feel so clean!" said Randy, our director), and the temperature and pressure were adjustable, but I wasn't curious enough to experiment.

We were visiting Tokyo to shoot a corporate film for a Japanese electronics manufacturer. Our plan was to shoot all the interviews in front of a 12' x 12' green fabric background we had brought from the States with our video gear. During post-production, video images relevant to each person's occupation would be matted into the green background.

With Carole, our local production manager, we scouted locations for these green-screen set-ups. In particular, we needed a place to interview an important client of our clients, Mr. Sato, a strategic ally who was an executive from a cell phone company. We visited his corporate headquarters, rode in an elevator larger than my living room at home, passed through several floors of security, marble lobbies, and greetings from underlings, and ended up surveying a large conference room full of leather couches, stuffed chairs, glass coffee tables, phones, stereos, and tall windows, on the 33rd floor of their office building.

"What do you think, Bill?" asked Randy. "It's your call." As the cameraman in our little group, I was the reality check. Was it really my decision whether we shot there or not?

"My call?" I echoed, contemplating how to empty this crowded room, and how to get our lighting truck and gear and crew in through the small garage of this huge building, then worm all our stuff up through various slow transport to 33.

"My call is, let's rent a studio, or a banquet room in a hotel nearby, where we start out empty, have more control, and have him come to us."

"Can't do it," said Larry, our producer. "They won't ask Mr. Sato to leave the building." Our three Japanese clients shook their heads in unison. No surprise there. They were always reluctant to impose on their clients, even when it obviously made sense for our production. "Gotta shoot here."

"Then in what way is it my call?" I asked rhetorically. It was feasible for us to shoot there, but only if we had access three hours ahead to strip the room of its contents, black out the tall windows, and set up our lights, the 12x12 green screen, Sony HDW-700A camera, audio, dolly, and track. And the occupants of the 33rd floor, all clients of our clients, had to understand that furniture would be piled up and down the halls, so we could transform a luxurious meeting room into an empty studio. Though we would act with respect and care and put it all back when we were done, it wouldn't be pretty.

To my amazement, everyone agreed to these conditions. The young lady who was our liaison with this client of our clients was surprised that we needed so much time and would be so disruptive. I was sure she had been thinking the interview crew would consist of one guy with a light on top of his camera, but they hadn't brought us 5000 miles to shoot news style.

Several days after our scout, Noburu dropped us off at the location, to stage an assault with our usual small army. Randy, Larry and I rode up via passenger elevator with Carole and our clients. Jon, our engineer, arrived separately in a van with his gear and Ota, the soundman. They planned to meet our lighting truck in the basement loading dock and come up through the freight elevators with our gaffer Hiyeda, head of the lighting crew.

We arrived outside our location on 33 at T-minus three hours and five minutes, but the conference room was occupied by a high-level meeting of Important People. They refused to yield to us, despite our room reservation. Getting the gear upstairs took forever. Jon told me later, "The garage doors were too low for our lighting truck, which wasn't that big. And this is a new building! None of our crew seemed surprised.

"So the guys parked the truck outside and rolled the lighting carts down a steep driveway into the garage. Here each load up waited forever. There was only one freight elevator for the whole 50-story building."

With about an hour and a half to go, the Important People finally vacated the room, and we went to work. Our video and lighting equipment piled up in the halls as we moved out stuffed furniture and glass tables, but our crew quickly sorted it all out. Soon furnishings littered the halls in every direction. Despite the delay, or perhaps because of it, we set up in record time.

I started feeling confident that we would be ready on time and wondered when our subject would arrive. In walked a middle-aged, important-looking Japanese man. I assumed he was Sato, our interviewee ... and I almost fainted. As our clients bowed and fussed and fawned, I was appalled to see that he wore a well-tailored tweed suit of a lightly colored wool blend. The problem was the tweed, a tightly woven herringbone of black and brown and tan, which jumped out to my eye as a perfect moiré weave. Certain small diagonal fabric patterns interact badly with the pixel scan of video cameras, causing a "buzzing" look or wavy lines, which will vary and pulsate as the camera zooms in and out. Often this unsightly electronic interference moiré pattern can only be solved by a change of clothing.

My throat went dry as I contemplated this disaster. I choked a mute, hurried plea for help to Larry, who looked at me with calm curiosity, as if my vocal cords were disintegrating before his eyes. I croaked to him about the "man in the moiré suit." He followed my gaze and smiled in realization. "Oh, don't worry, Bill, that's not Mr. Sato. That's Mr. Takahashi, the Boss of our clients from the company." I gasped with relief, curious to meet this über-client, who had been pulling the strings behind the scenes on our productions.

The real Mr. Sato, a handsome, surprisingly young executive safely attired in a stylish charcoal gray suit, walked in a few minutes later, amid more bowing and smiling from our clients. He was friendly and smooth and had a great smile. Randy interviewed him in English, and then, with a translator, in Japanese.

Carole told me later that Sato-san, after arriving and viewing the temporary destruction of his conference room, turned to our clients and said (in Japanese): "Wow, what a big set-up! Wouldn't it be easier to do this in a studio and have me come there?"

Now, why didn't we think of that?

Southeast Asia

Singapore:
No Worry, Chicken Curry

Getting to Singapore is a real butt-burner.

We skip across the Pacific like a flat rock on a pond, forced by full flight schedules to fly a circuitous route from San Francisco.

9500 air miles and 34 hours later, after plane changes in L.A. and Tokyo and a quick overnight in Bangkok, we land in Singapore's Changi Airport. By the time we arrive, we're wrung out. We're here to shoot a project for an American computer company as we fight stupefying jetlag and debilitating humidity.

After checking into our hotel, the modern but awkwardly named Raffles the Plaza, I bravely traipse out for a neighborhood walk through the thick air. I've been to Singapore several times before, and a short stroll reminds me how things have changed.

Years ago, in a park near our hotel, food sellers at Satay Garden, wearing pink plastic bags on their heads to keep off the driving rain, prodded us to order with great enthusiasm, pointing to each person in turn:

"Satay? Satay? Satay? Satay? Satay?"

"Beer? Beer? Beer? Beer? Beer?"

The satay guys are gone now. Singapore's ongoing construction and modernization have turned the park into an arts center and memorial.

On that same trip, we ate at the Banana Leaf Apolo Indian Curry Restaurant in Little India. Waiters slapped down huge banana leaves on the table, then presented the verbal menu: "Rice?" "Chicken?" "Vegetable?" "Curry?" "Fish head?" Nod your head, and they would slap large dollops of your choices on your banana leaf, which served as place mat and plate.

We ate with our hands, Indian style. No utensils. I strained to remember the Asian hand rules I had read in *King Rat*: "Right hand, food hand. Left hand, dung hand." Or was it?

On my walk, I cross the street and enter the polished classic elegance of the original Raffles Hotel—arched walkways, white columns, burnished railings, and the Long Bar once frequented by Rudyard Kipling, Joseph Conrad, and Somerset Maugham. Raffles was a legendary 19th-Century watering spot in the old trading port, an exotic setting for intrigue and romance in many stories and novels, and the home of the Singapore Sling. When I first visited in 1975 to shoot a travel film for Pacific Delight Tours, the original Raffles was a rundown, seedy symbol of the decline of the British Empire. Now restored, it is the flagship of an international hotel chain.

The humid weather is about the only thing that hasn't changed.

The Banana Leaf Apolo is still open, but over the years, Singapore's government has systematically destroyed ethnic neighborhoods and replaced them with high-rise apartments. As a result, most of the city is modern and bland.

Nevertheless, Singapore is a favorite destination for Americans and other Westerners for its lush greenness, cleanliness, and shopping, great for gringos who don't really like to visit other countries.

Returning to our current hotel, Raffles the Plaza, I explore the attached five-level Raffles City Shopping Center: Mont Blanc, Lego World, the Museum of Modern Art Store, Mrs. Fields' Cookies, Burger King, Orange Julius, electronics stores, restaurants and food courts, banquet halls and ballrooms for weddings and other events, even a supermarket in the basement. The air is chilled to a temperature that could keep ice cream at a thick consistency. In one corridor called Peacock Alley, I'm sure I can see my breath as I hurry through, shivering. Maybe that's a good thing: we're only 120 miles from the Equator, and outside, the muggy swampy air is unrelenting.

The day after arrival, we scout locations for our current shoot. Our local crewmembers reflect the cultural smorgasbord of Singapore. Lighting gaffer Krishnan, who owns a truckful of lights, grew up here after his parents emigrated from Chennai (Madras), India. Grips Malik and Sam are brothers, two of fifteen children of a Thai father and Yemeni mother. Tan, our soundman, is Chinese. Adam, local production coordinator, is a Bostonian, by way of Hawaii.

Our director Randy and I have worked with Krishnan and Malik before.

With a chuckle, we recall an earlier shoot, when Randy was spouting off to no one in particular about how bizarre it was to work with some corporate executives, middle-aged "suits," who liked to drop hip phrases like "Let's get it on!" "Awesome!" and "Time to rock and roll!" With little prodding, I had convinced Malik—a bundle of productive energy and impish good humor—to call out in his sing-song voice as we started the camera, "Okay, R-r-randy, let's r-r-rock and r-r-roll!" Randy was speechless with surprise, if only for a moment.

This time, we're here to film computer hard drive production in sterile cleanrooms, where workers cut, polish, and assemble tiny, delicate parts with sanitized machines. For one day's shooting we will have to dress in white "bunny suits" that cover all body parts except the eyes. The specs are strict, with an allowable contaminant level less than one part per thousand. I am always surprised that they let riff-raff like us into places like these, even after we swab down our gear with alcohol.

Our producer Larry is concerned that the rolling camera dolly we rented has crusty blotches of rust and corrosion; if the cleanroom supervisors won't allow it in, all our shots will be static. "No worry, chicken curry," says Malik, and he wraps the dolly in Saran Wrap to pass inspection.

I'm a big guy, and my worst problem with bunny suits in Asia is sizing. On a previous trip, the largest suit available was much too small, and I couldn't get it on over my clothes. Our producer took me aside and advised me to go to the men's room, remove my jeans, and force the suit on over my underwear. This suggestion made it possible to squeeze in my parts, but it was so tight I feared gangrene. Randy commented that I "looked like Nureyev on steroids," a sausage packed into a casing much too small. I'm sure even a cursory inspection would have revealed both my gender and my religion, and the effect—perpetuated by a treacherous photo taken by one of my companions—had been a source of amusement to them in the decade since.

This time we bring several extra-extra-large bunny suits with us from our client's facilities in California. But our Singaporean contacts cluck that these are the wrong type for their cleanrooms, and it looks like I'll be a stuffed *derma* once again.

There's a lot not to like about bunny suits. Nothing breathes. Our heads are covered with hairnets and nylon hoods, our noses and mouths with surgical masks, our feet with nylon booties, and our bodies with nonlinting nylon jump suits, rubberized at the ankles and wrists. Rubber gloves complete the ensemble, just in case some ventilation might slip through and the discomfort isn't total. Even the heavily refrigerated cleanroom air doesn't help: I feel like an overcooked kielbasa.

To add to the anxiety, Adam describes in excruciating detail the unpleasant experience of sneezing in a bunny suit on a previous shoot. Oy. *What could be worse than that?*

The night before cleanroom day, I encounter something more dreadful to anticipate in a bunny suit than a sneeze: diarrhea. In ultra-clean Singapore, where everyone drinks the water and food is usually safe, I contract the trots, the gastrointestinal problem known variously to international travelers as *la turista*, Bali belly, or Montezuma's revenge.

Fortunately, Imodium is a wonder drug, and by morning, I am sufficiently plugged up to avoid disaster in the cleanroom and more years of teasing from Randy and the boys. Unfortunately, I make the mistake of mentioning my affliction to our crew. Malik is sympathetic, enthusing, "Oh, I hate those wide-angle squirts, man, they're awful. Like chunky peanut butter!"

For the rest of the shoot, I address him as Chunky. Somehow, in my jetlagged state, this helps preserve my dignity.

Surprisingly, the suits prove less awful than my worst memories. I manage to jam my orthotic insoles into the booties, which are two sizes too small, and that attenuates my discomfort index somewhat. Surrounded by hundreds of similarly attired workers, we trudge slowly through the sterile factory over the next eight hours, like astronauts on the moon, methodically filming the newest automated robotic hard-drive assembling equipment. As we set up each shot, we blast the shiny metal machinery in this high-tech facility with colored light, creating interesting glints and reflections for our camera.

My biggest problem is recognizing my colleagues. The factory's engineers wear blue bunny suits, and the systems technicians wear green. But most of the workers are sheathed in white, like us. Few Singaporeans reach my six-foot-four elevation, so I am easy to distinguish. But from my point of view everyone else is, well, shorter. No hair is visible, so I learn to identify people by their eyes, brows, and glasses.

The plant is noisy and active. We are 16 hours ahead of our home time zone, and the shift in our daily body rhythms causes us to tire as this time travel takes its toll. Larry has his hands full, working out the logistics of our constantly shifting schedule, logging shots, and making sure we ID all our scenes accurately. Periodically our engineer Jon is forced to leave the cleanroom to change his mask, which has become soaked with the drippings of a bad cold. Randy marches us through from section to section, documenting the disk-making process. We are buoyed by the good cheer and energy of our local crew.

Exhausted after our day in the cleanroom, I eat a bony chicken and dumpling stew for dinner at the food court in Raffles City. People everywhere are cheering soccer matches on TV. As we are shooting in Singapore, the final rounds of the World Cup are unfolding in Japan and Korea, the first time ever in Asia, and the Cup play dominates local media and gossip.

I recall a visit to Singapore with Randy in the early 90s to shoot the manufacturing facilities of a Japanese electronics company. By then, this island city-nation on the tip of the Malay Peninsula had acquired a repressive reputation. Huge wall signs shouting "Death to Drug Traders" greeted us at the airport, and stories of people arrested for discarding chewing gum on sidewalks were common. At lunch, Randy came back from the restroom amused by a sign that proclaimed "$100 Fine for Failure to Flush Toilet."

"But how do they know whether you've flushed or not?" Randy asked our local crew.

"They have cameras."

"In all public toilets?"

"Yes, and in building elevators, where it's illegal to urinate."

"But that means there must be thousands of cameras in this city!" Randy was incredulous. "Who watches all those cameras?"

Our friends shrugged and smiled. Later a few students we interviewed stumbled over questions about their dreams for the future.

"You must understand," said one wearing a *Relax-la! Singapore!* T-shirt after we shut off the camera. "In Singapore, we have no dreams. Society is very regimented. We just do as we are told."

On another visit, just before we left for home, our local production manager treated us to a diatribe about political conditions, super-expensive housing, and 250 percent import duty on cars. Gas cost more than double what it sold for a few miles away in neighboring Malaysia, but Singaporeans were prevented from gassing up there. Political dissent was illegal and virtually nonexistent. One day he attended a small protest rally and found the police at his home afterward, waiting to bring him in for questioning. Around this time, the son of an American diplomat was caned for vandalizing a car.

After the bony stew, I return to my room to watch another soccer match with the door to my balcony open. When Korea scores a goal, I hear cheering both from the TV and from outside. About a mile away on the horizon I see lights—thousands of fans are watching the game broadcast live at a stadium there, excited that Korea has advanced further than any Asian team in World Cup history.

In two more days of filming, we document the installation of automated assembly equipment in this "factory of the future."

As a nod to Singapore's multicultural society, we feature workers of various ethnicities. Some of the Malay women wear Muslim headscarves, and the Indian women have distinctive makeup and jewelry. Most of the workers are Chinese, the dominant group in Singapore economically and politically, and their dress and attitudes are as Westernized as if we were in California. It's impossible to avoid the realization that the machines in our film will eventually replace many of these folks.

On most international shoots we do "flavor shots," exterior filming to provide a visual and cultural context, but not this time. The robots are the story. Randy and Wayne, our executive producer, grimly joke that, from our clients' point of view, the title of the film is *People Bad, Robot Good.*

On our last day of shooting, we wait hours for the factory engineers to get their new automated machinery working. *Robot Bad.* Malik amuses us with a naughty joke about a man from Singapore who visits New York. When he tries to order food in a restaurant, the waiter brings him a frankfurter. Confused, he asks, "What is this?"

"Why, that's a hot dog," replies the waiter.

"Ah," he says. "We eat dog, too. But we usually throw that part away."

The day drags on, but we persevere, bolstered by a late afternoon caffeine jolt from a local coffee joint. Finally, after less than a week in Singapore, we wrap, say goodbye to our local guys, and pack for the trip back home. Just as our bodies have finally adapted to the time change.

That night, our clients treat us to dinner at *Prego,* the Italian restaurant in our hotel. I order linguine with marinara sauce dusted with parmesan, and Caesar salad. Looking around *Prego,* I wonder: Am I really in Asia? Singapore has become so Westernized and colorless—"deflavorized," in Randy-speak—that we could be anywhere.

For dessert, I head to the supermarket in the Raffles City mall for Haagen Dasz ice cream. I realize as I pack that I have hardly been outdoors in seven days in Singapore. Except for my initial walk through the neighborhood, I have not left the air-conditioned cocoon of the hotel, the shopping center, and the passenger van that takes us daily to the chilly factory. Most evenings, we return from work tired, with little desire to go out on the town.

Krishnan has assured us that vestiges of colonial life like the Padang Cricket Ground and ethnic enclaves like Little India and Arab Street are still intact, and that public outcry saved Chinatown when the government proposed tearing it down. I wish I had gotten out to see these sights again, but my focus here was the factory of the future, not the city.

Next morning, I grit my teeth as we anticipate reversing our roundabout route back to California. I meet our engineer Jon in front of the hotel to load 19 equipment cases and suitcases and head for the airport, and I ask with mock alarm, "Where's the 17-inch monitor? We must have left it at the plant!" A harmless joke—the monitor is obviously sitting on the sidewalk in its huge shipping case, a foot from Jon's leg. But he was up late organizing and packing the video gear, and his stunned expression bespeaks his befuddled exhaustion. No worry, I think, chicken curry.

We shuttle back to Changi to check in, three hours before flight time. Contrite over my bad joke, I drag Jon to the airport Starbuck's to treat him to the corporate coffee of his choice. The clerk greets us, "Hey, guys, what'll you have?"

Iced grande latte and biscotti in hand, I feel as if I never left home.

UK | Japan
USA | Mexico

He has an incapacitating neuromuscular disease, where he has lost control of his body.

Health:
Our Most Important Product

Technology companies around the world spend megabucks each year on media for marketing. Here in the San Francisco Bay Area, for decades, the bread-and-butter work for freelancers like me has come from Silicon Valley's hearty appetite for film and video projects.

On a personal level, helping to sell some types of technology is much more fulfilling than others. *Enterprise application integration* or *managed hybrid cloud-based solutions* don't exactly tug at my heartstrings. No emotional attachment, no satisfaction.

With my kids grown up, losing both my parents (and a few of my peers) leaves me with a newfound awareness of my own mortality. More than ever, I appreciate that *health* is the most vital product of technology, more than my smart phone, tablet, laptop, satellite TV, digital cameras, or other beloved gadgets. Nothing ranks as high.

On a professional level, compelling, patient-centric healthcare stories usually fascinate—more so than talking head interviews with executives, engineers, marketing specialists, or software designers, which pay the rent but don't inspire.

Patient stories rely on real people talking about their own life-altering experiences. I get emotional when I hear how lives have been saved, health enhanced, prognoses uplifted.

I've filmed many dramatic leading-edge medical procedures in operating rooms and catheter labs, where patients' innards are punctured, probed, scraped, scoped, drained, frozen, examined, expanded, ablated and irradiated, to correct and repair physical malfunctions and enhance healing. Other patients benefit from new therapies based on improved medications, smaller and more useful devices, and enhanced connectivity. Four patients from my recent health-care shoots each occupy a special place in my heart.

It's barely ten degrees as our rented SUV skids up the icy driveway, greeted by a dozen shepherds, one monster gonzo guard dog, a flock of 20 sheep used for herding practice, and a gaggle of ducks for comic relief and sound effects.

Ethel is 91-1/2 years old and lives with her daughter Flo, who raises sheep-herding dogs on this farm outside a small town in Colorado.

"Mom really appreciates being out here with me," Flo tells our small crew, as we shiver while filming her in front of the sheep pen. Yesterday we were in Phoenix, where it was 50 degrees warmer. Here it's a beautiful, sunny day, and bitter cold, but we've come too far not to shoot the farm buildings and livestock. "She really enjoys being out in the country and watching the animals and babies when they're born in the spring ... so I'm gonna do everything I can to help her stay here."

We head inside to talk with Ethel, careful that our zoom lenses don't sweat internally as they slowly acclimatize from way-below-freezing temperatures to the overheated house.

"I don't want to live in assisted living," Ethel says with a twinkle in her eye. "I have my daughter, and I feel that she needs me as much as I need her.

"Here at home, I can do what I want to do, when I want to, and if I want to."

Relatively spry for her age, Ethel nonetheless has a history of falls, requires access to oxygen, and needs to be monitored daily for a variety of conditions. Each morning, she uses a small interface box through her phone line, to input her weight, oxygen level, and blood pressure. She answers a series of questions about how she feels, how she slept, and whether her breathing is obstructed. A nurse at the other end, 200 miles away, keeps track of Ethel's daily entries and those of many other patients. If she notices anything out of the ordinary, the monitoring nurse will call Ethel or send in a local visiting nurse.

Ethel also wears a call button to signal for help. If she falls, the device calls Flo wherever she is. If she's not reachable, the next call goes to Ethel's health monitor in Denver, who can dispatch medical or emergency assistance.

A few months after our visit to the farm, we learn that Ethel has passed away. I'm sad at the news, but certain that living out her days at home enhanced her quality of life, with the assistance of her daughter and our client company's easy, sophisticated monitoring technology.

"I felt dizzy and sleepy during the day, and I just couldn't keep up," recalls Toshi-san in a Tokyo apartment, when we ask what drove him to seek treatment.

"On the way home from work one night, I fell asleep in a taxi. Then the driver woke me up and said I was not breathing." The incident scared him. He realized that he needed doctoring, participated in a medical sleep study, and was diagnosed with sleep apnea.

Toshi's doctor prescribes nightly use of a CPAP. Our client's Continuous Positive Airway Pressure machine is a small pump that pushes air through a flexible tube and mask into the patient's airstream. This keeps open the airway in the throat which can otherwise flap closed during sleep, causing interruption or cessation of breathing and often loud snoring. Toshi slept fitfully and woke constantly. Every night.

Sleep apnea patients' blood oxygen levels can drop precipitously at night, a dangerous condition. With CPAP treatment, patients can breathe deeply, sleep longer, lower blood pressure, and decrease risk of strokes, diabetes, and heart disease.

Using the CPAP every night has helped Toshi-san immensely. For the first time in years, he is sleeping well on a regular basis, and his sleepiness, dizziness, and disorientation during the day have vanished.

He takes us out one evening to a favorite club.

"After work I have so much energy now. I enjoy karaoke with my friends. They all love my Louis Armstrong."

He scoops up the mic and croons a few verses of "It's a Wonderful World:"

"I see trees of green, red roses too. I see them bloom for me and for you. And I say to myself … it's a wonderful world."

Bud is 28, lives in Manchester, England, England, has completed university, and holds a demanding job as an actuary. He jogs in the streets, works out at a local gym, and has just bought a downtown flat with his fiancée, Robin. Remarkably, Bud has cystic fibrosis.

"He has led quite a normal life," says the doctor who has treated him since childhood, "counterpointed by cystic fibrosis, for which currently there is no cure."

A chronic, life-threatening, genetic disease of the lungs and digestive system, CF has long been considered a condition found among children. Seventy years ago, a newborn with CF would likely not live beyond his first year. Today, advances in medical research and treatment have extended the average life expectancy of babies born with the disease to 37 years. Planning a future is now much more feasible.

Bud is out to beat the average. Like any couple in love, he and Robin look forward to sharing their lives together.

"The most important and exciting thing in my life right now is Robin, and our flat," Bud tells us with a big smile. "That Robin was willing to make this commitment, knowing everything she knows about me, was huge."

"It's really great to own our own place," she agrees. "It's quite a big step. It's brilliant!"

One of the reasons all this is possible: Bud uses a portable nebulizer made by our client company, which makes daily delivery of his inhaled medication easier than ever.

Most CF patients are on antibiotics of some kind, and many therapies involve inhalation of medication to keep the airways open. When Bud was a boy, his nebulizers were heavy and archaic, sat on a counter, made a loud racket, and required electricity. His new nebulizer is a bit larger than a deck of cards, portable, handheld, silent, and battery-powered. For someone who needs to breathe in medication for an hour or two a day, this is a miracle. He can do his inhalation therapy at work, without disturbing those around him.

"I've seen a lot of positive changes in my lifetime with respect to cystic fibrosis," Bud says happily. We follow him and Robin to a pub one evening, where they meet up with friends.

"He tries to stay positive all the time," Robin says of her man. "He's just great fun to be around, and I can't really imagine my life without him in it."

"When I'm asleep," Ishmael tells us, "I dream that I am playing soccer on a soccer team and I score a lot of goals."

But Ishmael is 15 and has an incapacitating neuromuscular disease that is causing him to lose control of his body. His father, a Mexico City cabdriver, carries him up and down two flights of stairs to their apartment. His mother spends hours each day massaging and stretching Ishmael's limbs to keep them flexible.

Several times a week, his loving parents schlep him across the sprawling city for treatments at Teleton, a local charitable foundation that maintains a dozen clinics across Mexico for 24,000 needy children with chronic diseases and disabilities. At the clinic, Ishmael uses a cough assist device made by our client to help him clear his lungs of phlegm buildup, an interactive virtual skiing game where he can schuss and slalom down a mountain by swaying his upper body back and forth in his wheelchair, and a walking machine to keep his legs limber.

His disease has no cure. The treatments attempt to stay ahead of this degenerative killer, and the pace of Ishmael's decline has slowed markedly since he began coming to the clinic. Tragically, he was still ambulatory when his family first sought help at Teleton, but he lost the ability to walk during his three-year stint on the waiting list.

This type of conundrum presents a dreadful challenge to modern medicine. "Certainly, we can often perform miracles," a physician once told us on camera, "but these therapies are all fabulously expensive. No one can afford them unless they're rich or have the right insurance. But *everyone* should have access to quality medical care."

You might expect Ishmael and his family to be bitter about his situation.

"But despite all this," says his doctor as she suddenly weeps on camera, "he is a young boy who is seeking the deepest meaning in life."

"He dreams of being able to walk," says Ishmael's mom, also close to tears. "But he always says, 'Mom, since I know that may not be possible, my biggest dream is to be a person who isn't afraid of life.'"

At the end of our interview, we ask Ishmael if there is anything he wants to add.

"Thank you for giving me this opportunity to show what my life is like," he says as we all grow misty-eyed. "Thanks for making this film so that people in other countries can see me, which is something that I never imagined.

"I would not change my life."

These patients' stories elated and saddened me. I admired Bud's forward-looking spirit and Ishmael's philosophical perspective. But I felt personal connections with Ethel and Toshi and their healthcare.

At the time I met Ethel, my own elderly mother was still living alone in Arizona. Though Mom was in sparkling good health, my sister and other family close by, she was 96, and I couldn't help comparing their situations. Mom didn't need daily monitoring, but Mom had also had a few falls, a matter of great concern for all of us in the family. Like Ethel, she loved her independence and refused to consider assisted living. And like Ethel, she wore a call button when she was alone in the house.

With one difference: Ethel's call button, made by our client, a medical technology company, had a motion sensor that could *detect* a patient's fall and automatically call for help. I knew Mom had fallen a couple of times and, in her shock, *forgotten* to press her button, so Ethel's newer device seemed like a great improvement. Soon we bought Mom a new call button with motion detector.

Like Toshi-san, I have severe sleep apnea, diagnosed several years ago. I probably had sleep apnea for years or decades without knowing, or at least without acknowledging my problem. I slept very badly, waking many times during the night. Though never dizzy like Toshi, I was often tired during the day, able to drop off easily during car rides, to the amusement of my travel companions. My wife had told me for years that I snored badly and often stopped breathing at night, but I remained in deep denial until my sleep patterns grew so bad I had to do something.

The CPAP changed my life. I still wake up during the night, but not every hour, as I did before finally seeking treatment. I am less sleepy and have much more energy during the day. The machine is small and portable and travels easily. Over the past several years, I've taken it on international shoots and pleasure trips on four continents.

When I was a kid, General Electric's TV spokesman, future President Ronald Reagan, often uttered their slogan, "Progress is our most important product."

I've filmed lots of progress—hundreds of projects for tech companies: forward-thinking vision videos with actors in complicated, futuristic, dramatic or comic narratives; "big iron" films that show off the latest computer, tablet, monitor, phone, or server hardware; customer success stories featuring happy clients of our clients; software films that sell endearing enterprise solutions like *scalable content management, robust diagnostic tools, branded B-to-B services,* and *intuitive user interfaces.*

But promoting personal health is more satisfying than pimping the latest consumer gadgetry, corporate marketing, or social networking. The most rewarding projects in my career show ordinary people—trying to get healthy, stay healthy, remain in their homes, and live longer and better. Maximizing access to health care is the ultimate progress, and that truly is our most important product.

Taipei

Taiwan:
Mr. Wong and the Universal Language

An old joke:

What do you call someone who speaks several languages? A polyglot.

What do you call someone who speaks two languages? Bilingual.

What do you call someone who speaks one language? An American.

That's me.

I admit it: I'm only fluent in English. I'm a monoglot.

It's not as if I haven't tried. I studied German in school. My parents mistakenly thought I would become an engineer, and my mom signed me up for German, which she mistakenly thought was the best choice for engineers. An obedient kid, I studied German for five years in high school and two years in college. But for decades thereafter, though it occasionally helped me understand some Yiddish phrase, I never spoke German.

Much later, on three different shoots in *Deutschland,* I was reluctant to trot out those long-buried language chops. Back in school I could carry on a decent, simple conversation about a fictional life with *Onkel Klaus und Tante Gretchen,* the poems of Heine, and the tributaries of the Rhine: *Bei Schaffhausen bildet der Rhein einen Wasserfall!* But those synapses no longer fired. Besides, my German crews spoke better English than I did.

My dad couldn't believe Mom signed me up for German. He wanted me to take Spanish, reasoning that as a resident of the Western Hemisphere I would have many more chances to use it. He was right. I had a girlfriend from Colombia in graduate school, and I live in and have visited Spanish-speaking parts of the world on many occasions: Spain (three times, including a month-long honeymoon), Mexico (numerous times), Chile, Costa Rica, Puerto Rico, and our local Gordo Taqueria. Also Brazil and Portugal, where knowledge of Spanish can be helpful.

A semester or two of basic Spanish as an adult has helped me work with Spanish-speaking crews: *Esta lampara alli a la izquierda, por favor!* Most of the time they don't laugh at my efforts to communicate in clumps of words resembling their native tongue, as long as I avoid bothersome subtleties and troublesome tenses.

I can also read signs, order at restaurants, and find public toilets, but communicating ideas in *Español* eludes my rudimentary skills. If only I'd studied Spanish instead of German!

I never studied Mandarin either, but one time in Taipei I discovered that there are many ways to communicate.

I was in Taiwan with a San Francisco-based crew, shooting a global corporate image film for a Japanese electronics company. Our assignment here: to document the Intelligent Highway, a pilot program on a ten-mile stretch of freeway through the heart of congested Taipei. Our main shoot would take place on the second floor of an office building some miles away, where a control room staff monitored a huge illuminated wall map of the Intelligent Highway. Colored lights and displays illustrated breakdowns, slowdowns, accidents, and weather, and a large bank of computers—manufactured, of course, by our client company—controlled the flow of information. Pretty hot stuff for 1993.

We scouted this nerve center with Mr. Wong, our lighting gaffer, a large, impassive man who spoke no English. We Americans spoke no Chinese, and my German skills were particularly irrelevant.

It seemed obvious to me that the electricity in the control room was inadequate for our needs, and I didn't want to plug our lights into the same circuits that ran the computers. I consulted Cindy, our local production coordinator and translator, a native of Taipei who had recently graduated from NYU with a degree in cinema.

"I think we need a generator," I told her. "We need to rent one and park it downstairs and run cables up from the parking lot." She conveyed my concern to Mr. Wong. No reaction. Did he hear? Did he know this already? Did he care? She assured me he knew what he was doing, but she was just out of film school and lightly experienced herself.

We drove to the Intelligent Highway in a couple of Toyota vans, the Hiace models so ubiquitous abroad. Huge digital signs in Chinese alerted drivers of conditions ahead. Illegally and unintelligently, we pulled our vehicles over onto a narrow shoulder to shoot some footage of the Highway. A stiff wind shook my 16mm Arriflex camera, and cars and trucks rumbled by a few feet away. We implored Mr. Wong, Cindy, our director Randy, producer Jane, and our clients and drivers to form a windbreak near the camera. Rod, my camera assistant, sat down on the pavement under the tripod and anchored it with his body weight. Our combined efforts did the trick, and we were able to get our shots.

We wrapped hurriedly from the roadside and drove on to the lighting equipment company, where I asked again about a generator. Mr. Wong by now was starting to warm up. In the lot outside, he pointed out a huge generator he planned to bring the next day, assuring me in Chinese that it would be sufficient for our shoot. I crawled suspiciously around and over it as the daylight faded, trying to determine the capacity of this power plant. Without a flashlight, I couldn't read the small plate with the amperage, so I decided to trust his judgment and headed inside to the rental company.

We always hire local lighting crews and gear when I shoot abroad, and visiting the rental house is a must. Despite the fact that it was Sunday night, Mr. Wong, the manager, and several employees of the lighting company cheerfully endeavored—with Cindy translating—to help us finalize our rental order for filming the next day.

Here we encountered the Universal Language of Production.

From years of experience with international productions, most crewmembers abroad know a few basic lighting terms in English, regardless of their general level of fluency. On the set, I bolster this understanding with a bit of pantomime to get the job done. In a way, we all speak the same language, even when we don't.

I called in turn for each lighting instrument on our list. To see the 1200-watt (1.2 kilowatt) HMI light, I said slowly, "1.2 H-M-I."

The staff chorused, "Wan-poyn-too hay-tchem-aye, okay," and then brought it out, plugged it in, and turned it on. Frequent use and repetition of the Prime Validator "okay" are important components of the Universal Language syntax. We repeated the process for each light we had ordered. Many were ancient but serviceable.

"Wow, so this is where old HMIs go to die," said Rod. Yet they all worked.

Slowly we accumulated a lighting package, but several items had to be sub-rented from another company. "Are you sure we can get still get that?" I asked, always the Doubting Thomas. "It's after ten on Sunday night. Are they still open for business?"

The manager laughed and soothed, "No problem, no problem," a vital Assurance Mantra in the Universal Language.

Lighting control is as important as raw power, and I asked whether the lights came complete with scrims, as they would in the U.S. These circular disks of metal screening, useful for reducing the light emitted, fit into the gel holder slots on the lighting instruments. Double scrims are red, singles are green. A double reduces the light's output by half, a single by a fourth. The manager was puzzled by my request. He had seen those odd, round, useless metal things I described, but apparently he had discarded them.

How did they work without scrims? It was late and I began to get frustrated. Rod reined me in. "Just describe your need, Billy, and ask how they handle it." Good advice.

"You turn on light," I said slowly, in my embarrassing attempt to use as few words as possible. "Too much light. What do you do?"

Cindy explained my question. "Oh, endee, endee," they replied. Of course! ND! They used Neutral Density gel, a standard lighting supply. But how did they restrict light from hitting areas they didn't want to illuminate? Back home, we used black flags, 2'x3' metal frames covered with flameproof cloth. With common grip stands, these flags can be positioned to cast shadows as needed. Cindy translated, and Mr. Wong and the staff nodded. They had no full flags, but they did have empty metal frames, and they were willing to sew black cloth on them before our shoot the next morning.

"But what will that cost?" asked Jane, imagining an expensive Sunday night custom tailoring job. Wong shrugged, and the others smiled and shook their heads. We were already renting the frames and stands, said the manager. They would do the sewing for free.

By now we felt confident that Wong and company would take care of us. As we finished up late that Sunday evening, I wandered around the building, passing several sound stages filled with crews and actors shooting commercials and movies. Film production in Taiwan seemed to be booming.

I felt great. Clearly we were in good hands.

It was late and rainy, so we headed back to our hotel, the Ritz Taipei, and ate in the Chinese restaurant on the lower level—stylish, Art Deco, lots of black marble and silvery mirrors. At the bottom of the expensive English menu we read, "Prices above are for small portions. For medium-sized portions, add fifty percent."

We chuckled and tried to joke with Chen the waiter, who grinned gamely from ear to ear. If he didn't understand what we wanted, we pointed to the menu. It was near closing time, and we were his last patrons. The place was empty.

When we asked for water, Chen brought a large bottle of Pellegrino. The food was scrumptious, and we excitedly rehashed the day: the scout at the control room, the shots at the side of the Intelligent Highway, the scene at the rental company. Later, when we asked for tap water, smiling Chen brought and opened another huge Pellegrino. I drank a bit, but no one else was thirsty. At the end of the meal, we paid dearly for our medium-sized portions and got up to leave. I turned back to the table, grabbed the nearly full bottle, and said, "I guess I'll take this with me."

Chen jumped to help, and with a big grin, exclaimed, "Why not, it is you!" Waiters don't all speak a Universal Language, but they often come close.

Next morning, the breakfast smorgasbord at the Ritz was massive—table after table of omelets sizzled to order, bagels with lox hewn from enormous slabs of smoked salmon, ham, sausages, bacon, potatoes, bread, toast, jam, muffins, croissants, French toast, waffles, fruits, hot and cold cereals, *and* a huge array of Chinese food. Grab what you want. No translation necessary.

But I was worried again about our control room shoot. There was no elevator, and we had a lot to schlep up to the second floor. Before we could even start to light the scene, the generator had to be towed into place in a tight parking lot and cable wired upstairs. And we had a lot of material to shoot. The schedule was too tight.

My fears were unfounded. Mr. Wong brought his crew in early. When we arrived, the power plant was positioned and parked, the cables run, the lights, stands, and neatly hand-sewn flags were all upstairs, and the crew had breakfasted and was awaiting my direction. I was impressed. Mr. Wong shook my hand with a big smile. "Okay? Okay?" he asked, invoking the Prime Validator again. Okay!

I entered the control room, Wong and his crew following closely, and I showed them where to set the key light, a 2500-watt HMI with half-strength Color Temperature Orange gel.

"2.5 H-M-I, half C-T-O, bounce," I said, holding up one hand and smacking it with the other, to mimic the fact that I wanted the light bounced, reflected off a white card.

"Too-poyn-fye, hob see-tee-oh, bunts, okay, okay," they chorused. I used my feet to show position for each light and my hands to indicate height and direction. And so the day began.

We laughed together at my pantomimes. When shooting with a new crew in a new city, it's easy to tell in the first few minutes if they're up to snuff. These guys raced to set up the lights, position the camera dolly, and rehearse the shots. The morning flew by. It was fun.

At lunch, in the employee dining room, we were treated to noodles in a dishwater-thin broth. In fact, Randy pointed out, the soup was served in large steel vats that could roll around the room.

"When the meal is over, they just dump out the noodles, get rid of the ladles, bring out the mops, and use the soup to swab the floor," he said. "Clever repurposing." Keiko, our client from Japan, looked ill at the thought.

We returned to the control room and easily fulfilled the impossible schedule that afternoon. I shook hands with Mr. Wong and each of his crew and thanked them for their efforts.

"Okay, okay, no problem," they answered, conflating the Prime Validator with the Assurance Mantra. We couldn't have parsed complexities of Cabernet Sauvignon together or discussed the great dynasties of China, but we were able to communicate fully and do our jobs. Our shoot succeeded, thanks in large part to our common tongue, the Universal Language of Production.

We all speak the same language, even when we don't.

Sweet Home Shenyang

Sometimes we struggle to go somewhere. And when we get there, we wish were back home.

A medical client had booked us to interview a Prominent Radiologist in Shenyang, a bland industrial city of about four million in the northeast section of China formerly known as Manchuria, just 150 miles from North Korea.

From the beginning, Official China gave us problems. To apply for Business visas for my fourth trip to China, the four of us traveling—director David, producer Laura, video tech Jim, and I—presented ourselves in person at the Chinese Consulate visa office in San Francisco, along with passports, photos, visa applications, lists of equipment, and letters of invitation.

The visa office clerk behind the glass partition wore rubber gloves. She was friendly and tried to be helpful, but our situation was sufficiently unusual that she had to consult her bosses for long periods of time, as the four of stood in the hall. We could see them in a back office, poring over our paperwork, energetically gesturing and discussing.

Several times she sent us back to the waiting room for hours while someone else was consulted or some decision was made. At one point she told us we needed additional local invitations from our medical contacts in Shenyang, to prove our legitimacy. I wasn't sure why they were so cautious. Shenyang culminated weeks on the road for us, interviewing Prominent Radiologists in the Netherlands, Switzerland, Germany, the U.S., and Brazil.

All these countries welcomed our efforts to document advances in medical technology. As long as we followed procedures, there was never any question about them allowing us in. Mostly they were concerned with signing and stamping forms correctly. Rarely did Customs even glance at our gear.

China was probably concerned about admitting foreign news media who might publicize unflattering aspects of their society, and we'd been warned repeatedly that applying for Journalist visas would make them suspicious of us.

We reminded the visa clerk that we were making a film about new techniques in diagnostic imaging for a corporate client. "Not for television," we repeated over and over. Also, we had taken this same crew and equipment to Shanghai on a medical shoot for the same client just nine months before. Some of us still had those China Business visas in our passports. What had changed?

The clerk smiled slightly and admitted that the visa process could be "a little bit different each time." Eventually, after a couple of visits to the Consulate and hours of wrangling, they approved our Business visas.

Win! We had forced the regime to bend and admit our graying corporate video crew to extol the wonders of CAT scan and X-ray. Surely the worst was over.

But when we landed in Beijing a few days later, Official China threw a monkey wrench in our plans.

We had less than three hours to grab our bags from the carousel in the new Capital Airport, clear Customs, and recheck our gear for the eighty-minute flight to Shenyang. But Beijing Customs officials balked at admitting our equipment into China. A young man in his 20s in a fancy uniform had made this decision and would not budge. Period.

Great consternation! We showed our passports, our old visas, our equipment lists, our letters of invitation. In January when we entered in Shanghai, we had posted a bond of several thousand U.S. dollars for the gear. Did we need a bond again? Andrew, our Chinese fixer, attempted to translate and work it out.

He explained their ruling: the problem was with our Business visas. Our official invitation said we were entering for business *meetings*, not a video shoot. To bring in camera gear, they said, we should have had Journalist visas, the opposite of the advice we'd gotten at the Consulate in San Francisco. Last time, we reminded Andrew, the Business visas worked. Yes, he chuckled, but that was in Shanghai, where officialdom could be more ... flexible. Here in Beijing it was much more by the book. A little bit different every time.

Finally Andrew reached a deal. For the duration of our stay, Customs would impound our camera body—the most costly and prominent item on our equipment list—but we could bring in the rest of our 13 cases of video and audio gear.

We hated this compromise, but we had to make our flight to Shenyang that evening and meet a tight schedule over the next few days. And Andrew had already arranged to rent another camera body for us!

We staged an impromptu transition ceremony: I provided Jim a cheesy luggage lock to secure the zippered camera case. He handed our $60,000 Panasonic 3700 HD video camera over to the young Customs man in the fancy uniform. He locked it in a closet as Jim watched. In exchange Jim received a receipt, handwritten in Chinese, on thin shiny paper.

We were allowed to bring in our special lenses, camera controller, filters, video monitors, audio gear, and the EyeDirect mirror accessory that was so essential for the eyeline-direct-to-camera style of our interviews. Andrew arranged for a Beijing camera assistant to hop the midnight flight to Shenyang and bring us a rented 3700—the same camera. In a way, it was the easiest item to replace.

This minor setback wouldn't prevent our subversive group from interviewing yet another Prominent Radiologist!

After our battle with Customs in Beijing, we were very happy to arrive that evening in Shenyang. Right off the plane, jet-lagged and tired, we opted to eat in our hotel, the Kempinski, a German chain.

The ground floor held a Munich-style beer hall called the Paulaner Brauhaus. The idea of German food for our first dinner in China was too incongruous, so that night we dined at the Dragon Palace on the second floor. The food, though definitely Chinese, was mediocre and unimpressive, glutinous and bony.

So the second evening—after a long day trying to get our bearings, meet our principals, plan out our story, and shoot our main interview—David, Laura, Jim and I decided to eat in the hotel again, and by now German beer sounded good.

Entering the Brauhaus was like a trip to Munich, with an overlay of cultural clash. The menu was in German and English, the Chinese staff attired in Bavarian dirndls, lederhosen, and Oktoberfest costumes. We ordered beers and bratwurst and looked around.

The place could easily hold 300. Dark wood walls and furniture, brass railings and fixtures, shelves filled with personalized Paulaner beer steins belonging to regular customers. The Brauhaus was about one-third full, with both Chinese and foreigners sipping and munching. Shenyang's only micro-brewery occupied the rear of the hall. Clearly this was a local hotspot.

On a stage half way across the room, a band in tight green pants performed covers of American songs from the 80s and 90s—two girls and a guy out front singing and hoofing, two girls in back with guitars, keyboards, and a drum machine. Their volume was carefully mixed: the rhythms were loud enough to make you want to tap your toe, but the vocals were low enough that they wouldn't impede conversation. Saucy programmed lighting changed colors and patterns as they sang. Most patrons ignored them, and the dance floor in front of the bandstand remained empty.

Their voices were on key, as far as we could tell, their renditions of classic and near-classic rock songs inoffensive and pleasant, their dance moves efficient and skillful, if perhaps a bit ... bored. They were not Chinese. Someone said they could be Thai, but I had spent several weeks in Manila years before and I was sure they were Filipinas. Later they walked from table to table to greet the patrons, but we had finished before they made it over to us.

On the third night (after another long hospital shoot day, bisected by a huge, fabulous Chinese lunch feast), we opted for the Brauhaus again.

This time we sat much closer to the stage. We tried to order Martinis, but the waiters seemed unclear on the concept. They brought us Remi Martin cognac, which did contain many of the same letters. They sent over "the only German waiter" in the place to clarify our order. I could *ein bisschen Deutsch sprechen* with him, but I didn't know the word for vermouth and he wasn't really interested, so we settled for Paulaner beer. Again.

We ordered farmer salads and several kinds of sausages to share. When in Bavaria ... We did pass up the hog roast and knuckle of pork, authentic though they seemed.

We settled in. The same band, now dressed in white sailor suits with short skirts and high boots, was running through a repertoire similar to the night before. At a table near us, a tall, slender Chinese woman was swaying in her seat with eyes closed, quite taken with the music, her three friends gabbing and paying her no attention.

Later the band stepped down from the stage and started bumping and grinding unexcitedly on the dance floor. The swaying woman, overcome by the beat and the lager, joined them in a suddenly aggressive swing-waltz-tango that scared the entertainers back on stage. A couple of other patrons joined in a short dancefest.

After their first set, the musicians came over to schmooze. We thanked them for the music and learned they were indeed from the Philippines. Wistfully, they told us they'd been playing at the Kempinski for "eight months, so far," in a gig that could last a year. They asked where we were from, oohed and aahed because they knew San Francisco was beautiful. With a faraway look, one of the girls promised to dedicate a song to us in their next set, something to "remind us of home." But we had only been gone from California for a few days. Clearly *they* were the ones who were homesick.

After they left, we gossiped cattily. *They look older up close than they did onstage. More sweaty. Less cute.*

So snarky!

I'll bet a year playing in China sounded glamorous when they were back in Manila. Now they're stuck in Shenyang.

On the other hand, I had enough musicians in my family to know that a year-long gig was nothing to sneeze at.

What a backwater. Most people aren't even listening.

We never did learn the name of the band.

I started to wonder what song they would dedicate to us. They waved and smiled in our direction as they went back up for the next set. After two steins of Paulaner Hefeweizen, lyrics of nostalgic songs about my adopted hometown floated merrily through my brain.

Would they know that Otis Redding was "sitting on the Dock of the Bay" in San Francisco?

I could hear Clapton playing his sweet licks:

I got the blues from my baby, left me by the San Francisco Bay.

I could see Jeanette McDonald striding across the screen with Clark Gable, after the '06 earthquake:

San Francisco, open your Golden Gate ...

I could imagine Eric Burden and the Animals:

Walls move, minds do too, on a warm San Franciscan night ...

Then suddenly I knew what it had to be. A wave of homesickness did surge through me, though I'd just left home on Sunday and would be back there in a few days. It seemed obvious they would pick the song my beloved Giants played at every home victory. Everyone's favorite bit of Northern California nostalgia, sung by an Italian-American from Astoria, Queens.

I left my heart in San Francisco

High on a hill, it calls to me

To be where little cable cars climb halfway to the stars ...

That had to be it, right?

Wrong!

Which is how it came about that a Filipino band, in a Bavarian beer hall in a German hotel in Shenyang, China, in the former Manchuria, dedicated a song to their new friends from San Francisco—one born in Bombay, one in New York, two in California—all working for a Dutch healthcare company, and none drinking Martinis.

A familiar, toe-tapping guitar lick filled the hall. The other guitars joined in, then the keyboard, then the vocalists, in rousing, redneck-rock, Lynyrd Skynyrd harmonies:

Sweet home Alabama,

Where the skies are so blue.

Sweet Home Alabama,

Lord, I'm coming home to you.

A for effort and sweetness.

D for geography.

DC, LA, Cupertino

Steve Jobs:
Consuming the Apples

May 2001

The director introduced me. "This is Bill. He'll follow you wherever you go."

The host nodded at me. No rehearsal, no fixed plan, just stay with him, shoot whatever he says, and always try to show where we were. I slung the Sony F900 HD camera onto my shoulder, and we rolled tape.

He stood in a pool of light in front of a black wall, smiled, and spoke to the camera:

"Hi. I'm Steve Jobs, and I'm here at Tyson's Corner Mall in Virginia, right outside Washington, DC. I'm standing in front of this wood barricade we've built in front of our first retail store, that's gonna open in six days. Now, nobody's seen inside here yet, and I'd like to take you inside for a little private tour. So come on in."

He opened a door in the black wall, and I followed him into the first Apple Store, a week before its opening, gleaming like a bright new jewel with iMacs, PowerMacs, Titanium PowerBooks, iBooks, and no one but the two of us and a sound recordist. A huge photo of John and Yoko was visible at the far end. Steve beamed a proud welcome to the audience.

"Now, this is our store. The store's divided into four parts."

Then, pointing broadly to his left, "The first quarter of the store has our home section, with great home and education products..."

He stopped and glared at me. "You're supposed to pan over when I point there," he said.

Great. There we were, barely a minute into the tour, and I'd already pissed him off.

I had discussed what to do about pointing with Bill C, the director, and we had agreed that I would keep the camera on Steve. Later in the day, after Steve left, we would shoot cutaway shots of the home area and the pro section and all the other places he pointed.

It was a long, awkward moment.

Then Bill C came out of the back room where he and the Apple people were monitoring my camera and the audio.

"I asked him to stay on you, Steve. We'll shoot cutaways later."

"He should pan over when I point."

So we started again and I followed his points each time, then came back to him. We did shoot cutaways later, and some were eventually used to replace my pans that followed his gestures.

Steve Jobs was a world-class presenter and marketeer. But he was not a filmmaker. He had little patience for the deliberate, tortoise-like speed of most film or video productions. But the Apple Stores were a costly expansion, a new and risky venture. He wanted to film a video tour, and, unsurprisingly, he wanted to do it his way.

Our director had told us Steve's idea: that he would be alone in the store with a cameraman in the most low-tech setup possible: a handheld camera with an on-camera microphone, with no other crew, no lighting in the store, and no wires anywhere. He would start out in front of the black barrier, then walk through the barrier and lead the viewers through the store in one long, uninterrupted take. Simple, eh?

Except for a few challenges, which made our skin crawl as we anticipated them. First and foremost, no wires, at that time, meant that we had no control over the picture, that no one except me would be able to see and judge Steve's performance and my shots, and our director would thus be out of the loop. Of course, we could play back the video, but we knew Steve would never wait around for that, and we would have to get it right the first time. But if we could run a long, neat bundle of cables from my camera to the storage room in the back, the director, producer and our client from Apple could watch and listen. The on-camera mic was a bad idea too, so we needed to have our sound recordist trail behind me during the tour.

Another problem—the bright lighting in the store came from the ceiling. Were we really going to shoot this man in glasses, dressed in black, walking in a continuous shot through overly bright, white product areas, then into the dimmer, black-walled theater where his shirt might melt into the walls? This plan was destined for disaster if we let the auto-exposure unit in the camera control the brightness of our picture. But the lifeline cable back to the storage room would allow our video engineer to monitor the picture and remotely adjust the brightness, contrast, and color on my camera as needed.

To do this right, someone had to face down a man who was accustomed to getting his way. Meaning that our director Bill C had to suggest this methodology and convince Steve we needed to monitor and control quality. As a colleague of mine often insisted, "Don't give them what they want. Give them what they need!"

When he arrived, Steve grumbled about the camera cable and the soundman, but he went along, grabbing the lavalier mic and pinning it, without ceremony, onto the front of his turtleneck.

Continuing his tour of the store at Tyson's Corner, he showed off the children's areas, the racks of Mac software and accessories, and the new Genius Bar, a place to bring a computer problem or a problem computer. Sales and knowledgeable service in one place. Genius.

And so it went. We did walk around the store quite a bit on camera. We couldn't do it all in one take, so we cut and re-set between sections. In the Genius Bar, Steve told the audience, "I'm not a genius, but I'll stand behind here ..." At the back of the store, the theater video and audio hiccupped and glitched briefly as he switched modes. He grew angry about the glitch, called in an Apple engineer, dressed him down, and appeared to fire him on the spot. The man left quietly, but the following week our client assured me that he was still on the job and back in Steve's good graces.

But that day in the first Apple Store, after the glitch, Steve was done. Our client implored him to stay a few more minutes to shoot a wrap-up. He gave us a quick "I'll see you when the store opens" on camera, and he was gone.

We did pretty well. Control of the camera and audio in this very portable, impromptu situation that had to look and sound great, along with clever editing, and Steve Jobs' marketing genius, give the piece the feel of a seamless personal tour.

I had worked for Apple for years on a variety of film and video projects, starting in the early 8os, with talk show host Dick Cavett promoting Apple II and Apple III products. On one setup we had Dick walking around a huge bluescreen set, where he was composited onto a VisiCalc spreadsheet. A later film had Cavett pitching the very first new Macintosh, which sported "Lisa technology," referring to the point-and-click interface pioneered in that Mac precursor. Cavett needed coaching from our Apple client on the correct pronunciations of MacPaint (mac-PAINT, not MAC-paint, or mick-PAINT) and MacWrite (mac-WRITE). Nobody knew from Mac-anything, and we all had to learn.

In 1987, during the period of Steve Jobs' exile from Apple, I shot the Knowledge Navigator video, directed by my frequent travel buddy Randy. This prescient view of future technologies spawned a generation of "vision videos" through the 90s. Apple and many other high-tech companies produced grand visions, sometimes shooting 35mm film with union actors and mock-ups of wished-for devices and software interfaces in scripted, narrative films. A few years later I shot two half-hour future-tech films for Microsoft, a comedy and a murder mystery, one with a budget approaching a million dollars. The six-minute Knowledge Navigator video was widely distributed by Apple and then-CEO John Sculley.

I had been around Steve Jobs a bit, though I'm sure he didn't know who I was. I'd filmed him briefly at Apple a couple of times, but he had a prickly reputation and the crew was advised not to look at him or talk to him. Most of them were out of the room or behind a curtain while Steve was in the studio. Several times, we had waited all day for him to show up, eventually wrapping and going home, having shot nothing at all. And I knew other crews had the same experience. Some days, running two multi-billion-dollar companies (he was also CEO at Pixar) was more important than whatever promo message we'd been preparing.

I'd also been around him the day before shooting that tour at the first Apple Store, when I scouted the location with Bill C and the lighting crew for our film. We all felt the store was overlit. The overhead fluorescent lighting wasn't green or depressing in color, but the high-intensity tubes specified by the store's lighting designer were very bright, especially with white floors and walls. Worse, the computers were displayed on white tables and islands, and the intense overhead lights, to my eye, made the screens look dark. I was afraid they'd look muddy on video.

So we had experimented with removing the cover of one of the fluorescent fixtures and adding a layer of Opal Tough Frost, a light, white diffusion material we commonly used to soften lights. We wondered if anyone would notice this small change when the Apple people showed up a bit later.

Steve noticed immediately and asked what had happened. Bill C explained it was an experiment, to soften and reduce the overhead lighting slightly, so the screens could pop out better when we shot the tour the next day. Steve was interested in the idea and asked if there were different stages of softening available, and we introduced him to the world of lighting diffusions and showed him samples in a swatch book. He asked what metric was used to quantify the light, and I lent him my Minolta incident light meter and explained how to read the scale.

"So, it's logarithmic," he confirmed, grasping it quickly.

In the end, he had my lighting crew install Hampshire frost over the light fixtures, the very lightest diffusion available at that time, practically transparent. But when Apple rolled out the first few stores, the lighting looked just as bright as it had started out.

Apple was still just a computer company then, but they were already showing an awareness that the computer would soon be the hub of the digital lifestyle now so deeply engrained in our culture. Though the iPod was still just a twinkle in Steve's eye, the new Apple Stores sold digital video cameras and other-branded MP3 players. iTunes was already widely available, but only as a handy jukebox program for music you ripped from your CDs or downloaded from Napster.

My cousin worked at Apple at the time, and my uncle, a venture capitalist, wasn't sure if the stores were a good idea. There were many doubters in the business community. Business Week even ran a commentary the week the first two stores opened, titled "Sorry, Steve. Here's Why Apple Stores Won't Work." Now there are over 400 worldwide.

I was already a fanboy, having consumed more than my share of Apples.

I knew it could be difficult to see the new Macs, except in a few specialty stores, and software and accessories were not widely available. It all made sense. And now ten years later (according to a survey on retailsales.com in 2011), Apple stores are by far the most profitable retail real estate in the country, generating $5625 in sales per square foot each year. This compares with Tiffany second at $2974, Coach third at $1820, Game Stop fifth at $1009, Best Buy tenth at $831.

The week after the tour with Steve at Tyson's Corner, I was in L.A. to shoot the grand opening of the other new Apple Store at the Galleria in Glendale, California, another upscale mall. The Mac faithful came out in force. Hundreds of people lined up hours before the place opened at 10 am, and thousands waited on line all day to pass through and ogle the new store and all the product.

In the next couple of years, I filmed a slew of projects with Bill C, for Steve to show at keynote speeches at Macworld Expo in San Francisco just after New Year's each year, or at Apple product roll-out events in Cupertino. We interviewed Jonathan Ive (Apple's Vice President for Industrial Design) a number of times. We also interviewed U2's Bono (in Dublin), Aaron Sorkin (in his office at Warner Bros.), Annie Leibovitz (in her New York studio), Francis Ford Coppola (at his winery in California), Seal (in his LA home studio), Wynton Marsalis, Alanis Morrissette, Elijah Wood, Tony Hawk, Sheryl Crow, Drew Carey, Moby, and others. Dr. Dre stood us up three times.

We showed them the iPod; asked them about iPhoto, Garage Band, and the iTunes Music Store; or revealed the brand new swing-arm iMac to them on camera, dramatically pulling a black drape off the computer.

When we showed the guys from the band Bare Naked Ladies the swing-arm iMac, though, they thought it was funny and bobbed its head up and down as they made up words for it. Steve hated that. So on a Saturday night just before Christmas, the Apple folks flew us down to L.A. for an elaborate, substitute interview setup in a recording studio there, hoping our client could persuade Seal to drop by and talk on camera for a few minutes, on his way through town between vacations in Canada and Mexico.

"Steve would want us to do this," said an Apple exec as we waited around hopefully all day Sunday. Eventually that evening, Seal did come by to give us some great reactions as we pulled the drape from the iMac. He loved it.

I rarely saw Steve Jobs again, despite shooting many projects for him. His legend loomed ever larger, registering huge successes with each new product release. He led the charge into the digital lifestyle as Apple evolved into the giant, multifaceted consumer electronics, music, movies, books and software company it is today, the world's most valuable company.

The old hands at Apple, the ones on the original Macintosh development team, referred to Steve's legendary charisma and powers of persuasion (and never taking "No" for an answer), as the Reality Distortion Field. His powerful genius attracted many creative artists and persuaded them to become a part of Apple's legend and legacy. Annie Leibovitz told us he had called her himself to ask if we could film her, and Francis Coppola seemed genuinely surprised that Steve hadn't come with us to his vineyard in Sonoma County for the interview. As if!

See Steve Jobs' video tour of the first Apple Store at showdownatshinagawa.com

São Paulo

Brazil:
Some Days the Bear Eats You

The best laid schemes of mice and men gang aft agley.

My dad loved that Robert Burns quote. He would chuckle over the funny Scottish words, the unpredictability of life, and the way that plans could oft go astray.

When I was in film school at Stanford, our teachers pushed the idea that preproduction planning was the key to making shoots work, and I've always stressed intelligent forethought with my own students. You've got to have a plan going into a shooting day—a shot list, a logical order and schedule, a list of what you're hoping to accomplish and when—and the wisdom to accept that plans often change during production. Sometimes your planning gets trumped by outside forces, and your day gets messed up in ways you could never have predicted. You win a few, you lose a few ...

Mush called me from high up in the office tower.

"We're locked out up here!"

"Where?"

"Well, everywhere. I think the receptionists have gone home. I'm not even sure I can get back to you."

"Where are you?"

"I'm on the 26th floor, in the elevator lobby."

I was on the 2nd. Most of our gear was on the 26th, though we had left some lights and grip equipment on the 21st, thinking we would shoot there again. Every minute we stayed on the phone cost me two dollars, because my mobile plan was on international roaming here in Brazil.

"I can't get into the offices from here," Mush said. "The door is locked and I don't see anyone through the window. It feels like there's no one around. I think everyone's gone home."

Oy. Now what?

I had flown to Brazil for a week, to shoot and direct B-roll scenes (non-dialogue visuals) of people and technology for a Silicon Valley company. For budgetary reasons, I traveled alone, without a producer or crew. The production company I was working for in Berkeley had hired a Brazilian company to put together our locations, casting, crew, and other arrangements in São Paulo.

Mush's real name is Andrew, but he was nicknamed in childhood by older siblings. A friend and colleague of mine from San Francisco, he had married a Brazilian woman and had lived for years as an expat in Salvador, Bahia, about 1200 miles up the coast from our shoot in São Paulo. The production company had flown him across Brazil to work as my assistant, second camera operator, lighting gaffer, translator, bon vivant, and cultural attaché.

We needed shooting locations in fancy office spaces, difficult to find available for our midweek shoot days. So the Brazilian branch of our client company in California agreed to allow us to shoot in their high-end, high-rise, high-tech digs in the United Nations Business Center, a four-tower complex near the Pinheiros River. We scouted the tower offices on Tuesday, the day before we got locked out of the upper floors. The glassy, shiny décor and seeming accessibility of the offices were perfect.

An administrator named Cristina greeted us with a big smile, showed us various rooms and open spaces for our shoot, and pointed out the passenger and freight elevators.

From the elevator lobby on each floor, locked double doors led to our clients' office suites. Each door had a small window. "I won't be able to stay with you while you're shooting," said Cristina, "but the receptionist just inside can buzz you in when you change floors. And you can call me if you have any problems." We planned to shoot on three floors the next day.

The weather was beautiful and clear on that scout day. The windows in the tower had gorgeous views of the other tall buildings, and of the Octavio Frias de Oliveira bridge, a unique suspension span over the river. We wanted these dramatic backgrounds for our shots.

"What time would you like to start tomorrow?" Cristina asked Ricca, our Brazilian producer.

"When do you usually get here?"

"Always by 8:30 or 9."

"Too late," I said. "Can we please come in at 8?"

"Of course. I'll meet you here at that time."

If we get here by eight, I thought, *we can load in by 8:30 and possibly be ready to shoot by 9. Good plan. What could go wrong?*

That Tuesday scout day went very long. We checked out a dozen locations, and also shot time-lapse footage of traffic on sidewalks and overpasses near the main-drag Avenida Paulista, and from the roof of our camera van with my GoPro Hero camera as we drove around the city. At 8 p.m., we were still picking up tripods and other camera gear at the rental company, all the while plodding through ridiculous traffic in this sprawling metropolis of 20 million.

It was after midnight by the time Mush and I had eaten dinner, downloaded and checked our time-lapse shots, then charged, loaded and prepped our cameras for the next day. For some reason, I tossed and turned most of the night and logged little sleep time, finally tumbling out of bed at 6 to face the day, dragged out and ragged.

Ricca picked us up at our hotel at 7 a.m. Wednesday, allowing an hour travel time for our 8 a.m. call time at the tower. São Paulo traffic is often gridlocked but always unpredictable, and that day, by some miracle, we zipped along and arrived at location before 7:30, more than a half hour early. Our driver pulled over near the tower entrance, near a sidewalk with a typically South American zigzag mosaic pattern. Ricca called Cristina to get her ETA. Couldn't reach her.

I closed my eyes and dozed for a few minutes, then jerked awake. I prodded Ricca. Only five minutes had passed, but he called Cristina again. I dozed again, and we repeated this pattern for over an hour. At one point, I opened my eyes and squinted around outside. I looked up and saw our tower disappearing into the fog, then closed my eyes again. Around 8:30, Ricca reached Cristina, who was stuck across the city in stupendously bad traffic.

We tried to get in before she arrived, of course, but the building security people refused to allow us to sign in or even off-load our equipment to the sidewalk or the loading dock until they received authorization from Cristina.

"Have her call them from the car," I told Ricca.

He tried, but the security guys balked. The building bureaucracy (or "burro-cracy," as Ricca termed them, because of their legendary stubbornness) would only accept an authorization from a phone extension inside the building. "They say, 'How do we know it's her, if she calls from a mobile phone?'" She finally showed up around 9, her usual start time, and I wondered briefly if she had ever intended to be there at 8.

Cristina went to her office and called down to security about 15 minutes later. *Am I the only one feeling a sense of urgency here?* So after we had gnashed our teeth in the parking lot for the first 90 minutes of the day, they finally admitted our three vehicles to the loading dock. The entrance, it turned out, was nowhere near the tower where we were shooting, and our little convoy had to follow several service roads around the enormous complex. At one point our driver made a wrong turn and we all had to circumnavigate the towers a second time to find the way in. At the loading dock, a different set of security guys took a half hour to sign in our little crew of six, carefully scrutinizing IDs, inspecting our vehicles, and calling upstairs to reconfirm.

The security crew told us where to park and unload our gear, but after we had everything piled onto carts, we realized we still had a 15-minute walk—with our wagon train of equipment, through an enormous garage under the four-building complex—to get to the freight elevator of our destination tower. We had hired six actors for the day and would meet them inside.

It was nearly 11 by the time we attacked our first setup on the 26th floor, already two-and-a-half hours behind my projected start time. But now, clearly, the bad logistics were over, and we could start to work, flex our creative muscles, and zip through the shot list!

The setup started badly. Without taking time to measure the voltage, one of our crew plugged a Kino-Flo light into the wrong outlet.

Bzzzzzzp!

A spark, a loud sizzle, and a fried electric smell stimulated several of my senses, and an adrenaline rush, all at once.

"What happened?"

"I think he plugged it into the wrong place," said Mush.

"You think?"

"He burned out the ballast," the device used to control the special Kino-Flo fluorescent lighting fixtures used in film production.

"How is that possible?" I was incredulous.

"Well, there are several types of outlet plugs commonly used in Brazil, but the voltage might not be what you're expecting." Brazil has gone through rapid economic development in the past few years and is becoming a wealthy country, but "the electric wiring, even in new buildings, can still be ... surprising." To add to the confusion, each major city had a different voltage standard, and the government had recently chosen a new type of standard outlet.

We had other ballasts and thankfully no one was hurt, but it was an ominous and nerve-jangling way to start the setup.

I met the actors, whom we had cast from photos. One of the teenagers I had selected, for some reason, was not available, and the casting agency had sent a timid, pimply kid instead. Despite our specification that each of the actors dress for a corporate workplace and bring three or four changes of clothing, two had shown up with only the clothes on their backs, one in T-shirt and shorts. All this was annoying and limiting.

The scout day had been gorgeous, but the weather on our shoot day was hazy with low, foggy clouds. Our sparkling skyscraper and bridge views out the windows instead looked glary and white, with vague detail.

Nevertheless, we worked around the disappointing views and wardrobe limitations and cranked out four good-looking shots of people interacting with technology for our client company, a maker of Internet devices.

Our mission on this shoot was to provide shots of Brazilian-looking folks in Brazilian-looking locations, using iPhones and Droid smart phones, PC and Mac laptops, iPad, Galaxy, and other tablets, as well as teleconferencing and telecommunications equipment made by our clients. There was no dialogue, but the actors still needed my direction on what to do and how to react. Some spoke a little English, as did our crew, but Mush and I stayed joined at the hip and he and Ricca translated everything that went down.

Late start = late lunch. We headed down to the lobby, where we had to relinquish our security badges and sign out to eat at the shopping mall in the same building, then wait in line to sign back in laboriously after we ate.

Up on the 2nd floor after lunch, I got Mush and our crew started on a lighting setup in a conference room.

"And what are you going to do?" he asked.

Good question. I looked at my watch.

"Oh crap, it's close to 3. I'd better go shoot at the station while you set up." We needed shots at a train station, and there was an attractive one nearby, in the Brooklin Novo neighborhood. *New Brooklyn! I was born in Old Brooklyn.* We wanted to shoot at the station that day, because we weren't planning to be in that part of the city for the rest of the week.

We ran into Cristina on our way out.

"How are you doing?" she asked cheerfully.

"Doing well," I said. "Running around to make up for lost time."

"Well, best of luck to you. Call me if you need anything."

I ran off to the railroad station for a couple of shots with Ricca, the pimply kid, and the guy in shorts. Of course we each had to sign out and hand over our IDs again.

According to Ricca's research, the station authorities required an insane $5000 U.S. location fee, for shooting on the premises. No way! We only needed a few simple video scenes without lighting, so we had decided to steal the shots with my Canon 5D Mark II camera in a simple handheld configuration.

It was a bit of an adventure, as cops and uniformed security personnel patrolled both the Metro and intercity train platforms where we wanted to shoot. But no one noticed or cared. I slipped the camera into the station inside my backpack, pulled it out when the security people weren't looking, and grabbed a few shots of our actors without incident.

I used the 5D handheld with a short zoom lens and Zacuto viewfinder. No follow-focus, no monitor, no tripod. It looked like a still camera (it is!), and no one really gave it a second look, but I was shooting full-up HD video of our actors watching video, emailing, texting, and calling on their smart phones, with other commuters and trains streaming through the frame behind them.

I'm sure we were a circus to watch, as I yelled over the din of the station to direct them: "Look at the phone. Turn it horizontal. Now smile, and say something to the person calling. Okay, tap the screen. No, just once. Don't bang it, just tap it. Now look into the phone and listen."

As I yelled, Ricca would translate into Portuguese, and each actor would respond facially and emotionally. Some had never seen a smart phone before. If they didn't understand the directions, they would ask questions in Portuguese, Ricca would translate to English, I would respond, and he would translate back to them.

"Put it up to your ear now. Talk into the phone. Now hold it in front of you and pretend you're playing a game."

"What game?"

"A driving game, where the phone is a steering wheel, and you're speeding around a track."

Clumsy, but effective. We avoided the security people by working behind pillars when we could. After a couple of scenes on one track, we stopped at another one with a different look, grabbed a few more shots of actors, trains, and commuters, and headed back around 5:30.

We still had three shots planned at the tower, so we returned and signed in for the third time. It was August, winter in Brazil and now close to sunset. I joined Mush on the 2nd floor to see the setup. It looked awful. The windows were dark now and mostly reflecting the interior white walls. I couldn't bear to shoot it. It wasn't Mush's fault. Our late start had schtupped us at the end of the day. Also, Mush had been shorthanded. Apparently one of our crewmembers had been missing for hours.

We discussed a change of concept. Mush offered to run up to the 26th floor, look for our missing guy, and get a couple of lights and a different lens. That's when he called me from upstairs.

"We're locked out up here!"

"Where?"

"Well, everywhere. I think the receptionists have gone home. I'm not even sure I can get back to you."

At that point our gear and crew were spread among three floors. Big problem.

"Call Cristina," I told Ricca. "Find out how we get back in. Who do we call?"

He called her, then turned back to me with a frown. "She's gone for the day," he reported incredulously. "She says the offices close at 6. Period. There is nothing she can do. There is no one else to call." Oy! She hadn't told us that before, even when we had run into her during the afternoon. Had we known, we could have postponed the station shots for another day.

Ricca went off to investigate. After a while, he found the wayward lighting crewmember, chatting up our makeup artist on another floor. He also ran into a cleaning lady who offered to open some doors for us, but warned us we couldn't stay long. The building would be locked up tight at 8. I called my home producer in Berkeley (again, at a two bucks a minute). We decided to cut our losses and to pack it in for the day.

I took stock of the situation. We'd gotten four of our seven shots at the tower, plus the setups at the station. We hadn't met our ambitious goals, by a long shot, but we had acquired some good material. Much of our plan had worked. And yet, we had spent hours immobilized in exasperated frustration. How could we have predicted we would be squeezed for time at both ends of the day?

The cleaning lady opened up the 26th and 21st floors. The missing crew guy showed up all smiles and gave me a hug at the end of the day. We wrapped our cameras and lighting gear, skulked down the freight elevator, slunk back to the vehicles through the labyrinthian garage, and hit the streets.

Adding insult to injury, it took nearly an hour and a half to zigzag through São Paulo evening rush hour gridlock back to the hotel, a trip that had taken 25 minutes that morning.

Quick dinner, then bed. Tomorrow's a brand new day.

Some time later, Mush and I tried to analyze what happened. Could we have predicted or avoided it? Had the corporate culture let us down? Mush, who has lived there 20 of the last 28 years, thinks it could be something about Brazil.

"As a North American production crew, our expectations ran a course of time management prediction based on worldwide experience," he said. "But Brazil does not conform to those petty and predictable concepts. It is its own world with a set of rules shamelessly circumvented, while apparently adhering to them with a charming smile."

Perhaps. But long experience tells me that some days unpredictability reigns, even with the best of intentions. Some days the production gods are angry, and moving through a shoot schedule feels like slogging through waist-deep tapioca pudding.

Some days you eat the bear, and some days the bear eats you.

Less than an hour after posting this bad-day saga on my blog, a freelance coworker back in San Francisco responded: "Nice, Bill. Easy days are completely forgettable."

True that!

"But," he added, "I'm available if you've got any coming up."

After our tough time at the tower, the next couple of shooting days in Brazil were smooth as silk. As my friend predicted, I can't remember much. Just the broad strokes—what we did and where we did it. I can easily spin out 2000 heartfelt words to immortalize a tough shoot, but easy days often leave me with little to write about. It's difficult to find a dramatic narrative arc in a yarn about a happy, professional crew cheerfully moving apace from setup to lovely setup.

An easy shoot makes you feel like anyone could have done it. Overcoming obstacles presents a challenge, tests your mettle, lets you show what you can do ... and makes a great story.

Tokyo, Nagoya

Gigantic in Japan:
A Tall Tale

All I wanted was a shower and a snooze.

I had endured a crippling flight to Tokyo in a coach seat with knees jammed against the seatback in front, an interminable business dinner right after my arrival, and a harrowing drive, as my host ebulliently (and somewhat drunkenly) drove me into the city. Now I was finally alone in my room at the Creston Hotel near Shibuya Square, and I craved hot water unclenching my tired, bunched-up muscles, followed by eight hours in the sack.

I approached the shower drowsily, maneuvered the controls with clumsy, jetlagged hands, started the steamy cascade of relief, stepped into the stall, straightened up in the warm spray, and ...

BAM!

... banged my head on the ceiling. Dazed and glazed, I scrutinized the shower, a one-piece molded plastic pre-fab, three feet across, four feet deep, and about six-feet-three tall. Unfortunately, I'm six-feet-four. Clearly, I fell outside Japan's range of "normal" human height.

I've always been too tall for Asia.

In Taiwan one time, I happily bounded up four rickety steps to the men's bathroom at a film studio.

BAM!

I slammed my head into a low doorway. Suddenly I lay stunned on a damp floor, looking up at the urinals. A young Chinese man peeing into the trough next to me looked down with alarm and called out, "Okay? Okay? Okay?" in that loud voice we all use when addressing people who don't share our language. I got up slowly, squinting warily at the six-foot-high door lintel, four inches too close to the center of the earth. The peak of my ball cap had obscured this low doorframe as I watched my footing on the stairs.

In Manila on another trip, I towered over two young Filipino bellboys in white uniforms and chin-strap pillbox hats. They escorted me to my room, dragging my luggage down the corridor, then shyly asked if I was a famous American basketball player. "Yes," I responded solemnly, "I'm Magic Johnson."

In Singapore, China, and Japan, I had stuffed my ample body into cleanroom bunny suits and operating room gowns made for much smaller humans, a sausage-like effect. And I towered over my coworkers in crew photos all over Asia.

So my skull clanging against the shower ceiling at the Creston wasn't surprising. Japanese people had long been among the smallest in Asia, and I had felt like a Brobdingnagian freak there before.

On my first trip in 1975, I was sent to Japan to shoot a travel film. It was springtime, and the youth of the country were on the move. Schoolchildren were everywhere, flooding trains, buses, streets, and tourist destinations, and they obviously had never seen anything like me—skinny, shaggy-haired, black-bearded, and two heads taller than most of them. With my film camera on one shoulder, I waded through seas of black-uniformed students. Thunderstruck to see me but too polite to point, they stopped dead in their tracks, staring, laughing, waving. I chuckled and waved back.

One day we rode the train to Kamakura, famed for its many temples and home to the Daibutsu, the 43-foot-tall bronze Great Buddha, which has occupied hallowed ground there since 1252. I strolled around back and spotted some kids who had climbed up inside the enormous hollow statue and were leaning out a small window at the Buddha's shoulder blades. If the Buddha had had shoulder blades.

All the proportions were wrong. The children were small in a huge Buddha. I was large and towered above the kids around me like a giant out of Gulliver's Travels. When the kids in the Buddha spotted me, a hirsute gai-jin pointing a big camera toward them, they waved and called out "Ohayo! Ohayo!"

I was puzzled. I knew they weren't from Ohio. I resisted the temptation to yell back, No, California.

"Why do they think I'm from Ohio?" I asked our guide.

"They don't. Ohayo means 'Good morning!'"

Another time in Tokyo, my director Randy and I both scheduled shiatsu massages in our adjacent hotel rooms one evening after dinner. My masseuse, who spoke no English, went about her business stoically as she poked and pummeled my body into submission. But the wiry, gray-haired lady who came to massage Randy—who's about six feet tall—threw up her hands and clucked, "Too big! Too big!" when she first confronted him.

His reaction: "Hey, you should see my pal next door!"

I've visited Japan ten or eleven times in all, and we've both changed. My beard has been replaced by glasses that never leave my face, the long, jet-black hair has thinned and mellowed to a distinguished, close-cropped grey, the skinny frame has thickened with middle-aged sprawl ... and the Japanese people seem more accustomed to seeing tall foreigners. At least they don't stop and stare as obviously as they once did.

But some things never change. When I've gone bowling in cosmopolitan Tokyo, renting shoes evokes giggling apologies—"Ohhhh, feet too big!"—and a trip to the storeroom to seek out Godzilla-size clodhoppers. Salespeople come running if I enter a clothing store, waving me off and shaking their heads with embarrassment: "No fit, no fit." And folding these long legs under low tables in traditional tatami dining rooms is challenging at best.

Hotel rooms with facilities as small as the Creston—or even smaller—are ubiquitous. On a recent filming trip, I checked into a hotel in Nagoya with my crew. The lobby was suitably fancy, but as we walked down the 17th-floor corridor, I heard Randy mutter, "Uh oh, these room doors are much too close together." That meant one thing: tiny rooms.

He was right, and late that night, after dinner with our clients, we decided to have some fun. The result: "Bill and His Room: A Tall Story," a home movie far from home. Somehow Randy convinced me, after only one beer, to get in touch with my inner ham and be his star. The film starts on the street after midnight, a whistling version of "Sentimental Journey" on the soundtrack.

"We're here in Nagoya, Japan," I narrate on camera. "We came about 200 miles on the Bullet Train today ... I had to be very careful about bumping my head on the train door, because I'm six-four."

"Here in Nagoya, there's a lovely, luxurious Hilton Hotel. However [voice dripping with sarcasm] we're not staying there. We're here at the Nagoya Crown Hotel ... a salaryman hotel. Kinda small, definitely not made for people my size."

I walk up the stairs in fast motion as the camera follows, through the lobby doors (ducking my head), into the elevator, then down the hall to my door. I open it, touch my forehead to the doorframe without stretching, stoop down, and enter the tiny room. But how small is it?

My narration continues rapid-fire: "I'm about six-feet-four this way [height] and roughly six-feet-four this way [arm span]. If I stand close to the center, and touch this wall with this hand [comic graphic overlays of measured lengths], I am about three inches short of touching here [funny music], which means the room's less than seven feet wide."

Amenities? Quick shots of a small, old-school media control panel that looks like a stereo I had owned years before, a tiny television, and a window opening opposite a brick wall I can touch without leaning out. I don a hotel bathrobe and lie down exhausted on the bed, feet hanging way over the end.

Plumbing? In this small hotel room, the whole bathroom was a prefab, molded plastic compartment. A montage of shots: the camera trails up my body from feet, flat on the ground, to head, tilted to fit against the ceiling; I stand in the shower stall and touch both walls with my elbows; I sit on the toilet with my feet outside the bathroom; and I fold up—clothed—in the tub, my knees up around my ears.

This shortsightedness (pun intended) in plumbing fixture standards is not unique to Japan. In the U.S., showerhead pipes routinely stem out from the wall six feet above the floor, then curve downward (indeed, this height is the building code standard in many states). Though this aims the spray perfectly at that crucial area between my nipples and my navel, washing my hair in a confined space with a low spray requires a contortionist's skill.

But now Japan has changed. According to an article in The New Yorker in April 2004: "Americans haven't grown much taller in fifty years. By now, even the Japanese—once the shortest industrialized people on earth—have nearly caught up with us." And another story in the Oberlin Alumni Magazine agrees: "If you're in Asia today, the intergenerational differences in height are striking ... the Japanese ... have increased their height by about eight centimeters [over three inches] in the last 50 years."

That statistic refers to the average height of Japanese of all ages. Greatly increased average heights among young people in the second half of the 20th Century have driven up that national average.

An article by Howard W. French in The New York Times in 2001 states, "In 50 years, according to statistics kept by the Ministry of Education, the average height of Japanese 11-year-olds has increased by more than 5 1/2 inches. The height of girls, who grow faster at that age, meanwhile, has increased even more." I wondered when I first read this if the national infrastructure would respond to this generational height increase.

"But taller young people here complain that the Japanese idea of themselves as a short people has not kept pace with reality," says the Times article, "resulting in a frequently inconvenient mismatch." Such as banging heads on doors and ceilings.

Those 11-year-olds surveyed at the end of the century are now in their mid-20s and an important part of the consumer economy. "The old Japanese industrial standards no longer fit Japanese life," said a consumer researcher quoted in the Times. "The standard cooking table, for example, only fits the older generations. We are trying to measure the younger generation so as to advise Japanese corporations how to meet their needs."

So help is on the way. Changing the sizing of infrastructure is a slow process, usually accomplished over time as older buildings, facilities, and vehicles wear out and are replaced. Average height for men in the U.S. accelerated during the post-war era through the 50s, and then increased only one inch from 1960 to 2002, and less than that for women.

When I was growing up, I wasn't thinking about knee room in airline seats or low ceilings in Tokyo, but I was acutely aware that I had trouble buying pants in my length. I grew so rapidly at times that it seemed I was always wearing high-water pants. Department stores never carried the 34" inseam lengths I eventually needed, and a visit to a tall men's shop (the

Freak Store, according to a six-foot-eight friend) usually meant double the cost. Japan was starting to grapple with this problem decades later, when the Times article was written in 2001:

"The most obvious area where this mismatch is encountered is in clothing. Japan's clothing manufacturers still tend to offer few goods to those on the taller end of the scale. The problem goes well beyond clothes, though, and extends to furniture, automobile design and train seats, too."

Interestingly, Howard French, the Times author, added: "(A disclosure: at 6-foot-4, this reporter is familiar with the issue.)"

I wonder what has happened as the younger, taller Japanese confront an infrastructure built for earlier, shorter generations? Have they cracked their crania on shower ceilings (even as they wash thoroughly in the nipple-navel interspace), assaulted train doors, and smacked into restroom doorways as frequently as their tall foreign visitors? Do they curse their elevated stature as they hang off beds, squeeze into small tubs, dine on tatami, buy pants, and rent bowling shoes? Has Japan adapted and started to provide facilities and products for longer humans, or has this proven too tall an order?

Japanese people don't gawk at me as much, but I don't see too much evidence of tall-friendly change. In the half dozen times I've been back to Japan since the turn of the century, I have lost about an inch of height myself. But I continue to enjoy the genial people, the enchanting culture, and the delectable food—even as I walk around stooped over in constant fear of the big bang, and cramped from shoehorning into spaces built for earlier generations.

As I write this, I am prepping with my wife for a trip to the Netherlands next month. Since the Dutch are the tallest people on the planet, I assumed that I would be safe there, that the infrastructure would favor elongated people. But the Hollanders only reached their lofty heights in the past hundred years. The government has recently mandated increased height in doorframes of official buildings and made a few other concessions to tall folks like me. But this contrasts with most accounts of typical Dutch housing.

Years ago, I stayed at a bed-and-breakfast in a private home in Amsterdam, and I remember that the oddly angled, narrow, short-tread staircases were difficult to navigate, especially at night. In their book *The UnDutchables*, Colin White and Laurie Boucke describe at some length the small, crowded rooms and steep stairs in classic Dutch architecture, which dates from the 17th Century.

Then they add: "Nowhere is the sense of claustrophobia more pronounced than in the water closet. The Dutch have taken the term literally and made that most private of rooms the size of a cupboard. Once you've managed to get inside the thing, you then face the problem of turning to close the door and adjust your clothing.

"Before seating yourself, you face the dilemma of deciding whether you want your knees pressed tightly against the door or wall, or rammed under your chin."

Long legs + small space. Sounds familiar. Another "frequently inconvenient mismatch." For part of the time in Holland, we'll be staying on a barge in an 8' x 10' cabin with a two-meter ceiling height. Assuming I'm brave enough to stand upright, I should have a couple of inches clearance before concussion, but I still might feel claustrophobic. About the same as feeling gigantic in Japan.

See the film "Bill and His Room: A Tall Story" at showdownatshinagawa.com

Kampala
Entebbe

Uganda:
A World Together

Things weren't going well. We only had three days on the ground in Uganda, and our film stock, lights, sound gear, and local crew hadn't arrived. We did have our camera, however, and some borrowed film, so we could shoot people on the street and scenic shots here in Kampala, the capital. But that was it.

Moreover, Randy was grumpy. He snapped at me about the framing of a shot, a rare occurrence in our long professional relationship.

"Why are you so crabby?" asked Nancy, a nurse attached to our project as a client liaison.

"I'm not crabby!" he answered crisply. She looked at me.

I knew why he was crabby. For years he had teased me for having "a bladder the size of a walnut." I typically retorted that he rarely consumed enough liquids, that it was abnormal for any human to pee only on Wednesdays.

Uganda was the centerpiece of a seven-week, round-the-world, six-continent trip, shooting a corporate image film for a Japanese electronics company. We had arrived in Kampala the night before, after four weeks on the road filming advanced telephony in New Zealand, translation machines and kimono design in Japan, intelligent highways in Taiwan, and a software institute and computer assembly plant in Singapore.

During our endless, three-flight, 21-hour ordeal flying in from Singapore the day before, fellow crew members Rod and Jane and I had each gulped down several bottles of water and showered in the Business Class Lounge in Johannesburg between flights. Randy, our director, had done none of that. He was dehydrated.

"You're crazy," Nancy told Randy. "Those planes are as dry as the Gobi Desert. I'm shutting you down until you drink some water."

I blinked. *Could she do that?*

"Okay," he said, more timidly than expected, "and then there's the Lariam." The malaria medicine we were all supposed to take.

"What about it?"

"I took them all yesterday when we arrived, and I've been feeling lousy ever since."

"What do you mean, *all?*" asked Nancy.

"I took them all yesterday."

"You're only supposed to take one a week."

"I know. I misread the directions. I was a little groggy by the time we got to the hotel."

"Dehydrated."

"Maybe."

"You mixed up 'take one a week' with 'take them all right now?' Maybe that's why you've been crabby today?"

She forced him to sit down for ten minutes, get out of the hot sun, and drink a whole bottle of water. He regained his composure and we continued to shoot, though I knew we would tease him about this for years.

Solving the problem of our missing crew and equipment was more difficult. The day before, we had flown from Singapore to Johannesburg to Nairobi, Kenya, but the last leg of our epic journey—a short Uganda Airlines flight from Nairobi to Entebbe Airport near Kampala—was delayed by a downsizing of aircraft and change of seat assignments. Some passengers and luggage were left off the plane, including, unfortunately, our Nairobi-based sound engineer and lighting assistant, and all our rented sound gear. And that was the last flight of the day.

Our story in Uganda promised to be compelling. Our client company had donated a satellite communications system and computer equipment to the medical school at Kampala's Makerere University, to provide an affordable link to the outside world of medical research and technology. International phone and fax service were prohibitively expensive, and email was not yet in common use at that time. Uganda was isolated and poor.

We needed interviews to tell our story, and we couldn't shoot interviews without our sound recorder and microphones. So, with borrowed film but without sound, all our shots with my Arri 16SR camera on the first morning were scenics and people on the street.

That last flight from Nairobi the day before had been memorable for other reasons.

After sitting on the ground for hours, the plane was hot and stuffy, the seats were small, and we were thoroughly uncomfortable. Upon takeoff, smoke billowing from the ceiling vents of the plane startled us all. But we soon realized it was vapor condensing as the air conditioning fought a losing battle with the humid, steamy cabin.

A steward had brought around unappetizing cucumber sandwiches that seemed past their prime. "I hate this," said Randy, who had been dreading this part of the trip for a while. We had all traveled extensively in Europe and Asia, but Africa was a big unknown.

Just then Jane, our producer, passed him a note: "My vomit bag has been previously used." We laughed, the tension broken. I saved an unused Uganda Airlines sickness bag; weeks later, I faxed it to Jane and Randy.

We had flown across Lake Victoria, bordered by Kenya on the east, Uganda on the north, and Tanzania on the south. As we approached Entebbe at twilight, we saw a burned-out plane on the ground below, beside a destroyed terminal, remnants of an Air France flight hijacked by Palestinian militants in 1976. They landed at Entebbe with over 200 hostages and the support of Ugandan dictator Idi Amin and his army, then were defeated by Israeli commandos in the surprise Raid on Entebbe. The wrecked hulks of the plane and terminal building were left to rot, and a new airport was built nearby.

Seventeen years after that, we arrived at that new airport, by then a couple of decrepit, long, one-story buildings, where we met key members of our crew. Ian, our production coordinator, a blond, burly chap, was descended from Brits who had moved to Kenya in the early 1900s. Alan, our lighting gaffer, was a Londoner sent to run the Nairobi rental operation of a British lighting company, then cut loose when they closed their office there ten years before. Both were based in Nairobi. There was no film industry in Uganda at that time.

Ugandan Customs officials made a cursory check of our luggage. As it grew dark, we piled onto a one-hour shuttle bus to Kampala. Rod piped up, "You know, the State Department has posted a Travelers' Advisory that tourists should beware of the road from Entebbe to Kampala."

Uh, good to know. But how else do we get to our hotel?

"It's frequented by thieves."

Great.

"Especially after dark."

We appreciated the warning. Fortunately, no bandits attacked as we drove. The Sheraton Kampala stood behind a guarded gate on a hill overlooking the city, surrounded by manicured gardens in a walled compound—the center of an international whirlwind of activity to rebuild the country after the bloody, disastrous Amin and Obote regimes. Vehicles with logos from UNESCO and other relief organizations filled the parking lot. Several diplomatic missions had offices in the hotel, and at one point I rode the elevator with the Israeli ambassador.

It was an old place, with a rich colonial feeling—lots of dark carved wood in the lobby, bar and restaurants. We discovered the luxury of strong, dark, African coffee, after two weeks in Asia with wimpy, canned, coffee-esque swill.

The lobby was air conditioned, as were the hallways on the guest floors, but the rooms, oddly enough, were not. International phone service was expensive. A newsy, one-page fax to my family, which took one minute to transmit, cost $18 U.S.

Ian told us that the Sheraton, formerly known as the Apollo, had been used during the Idi Amin era as a center for interrogation, torture, and murder. This traumatic period in the nation's history had seen the liquidation of hundreds of thousands of Ugandans. And Milton Obote, who ruled both before and after Amin, was even worse.

At the money exchange, each U.S. dollar gave us nearly 1200 Ugandan shillings. There were no coins; the country was poor and had few precious metals. The hotel mostly had 1000-shilling notes, many worn, stained and ripped. Changing $100 US gave me 120 bills, a huge wad, and Jane ended up with a boxful for production expenses. Today the rate is about 2500 shillings per dollar, but larger bills are available.

Our borrowed film had come from Ian, as Eastman Kodak had bungled our original film order. Our home office in San Francisco had pre-ordered film stock shipped to Kodak in Nairobi, for Ian to pick up and bring to us. But he showed us a curious fax from Kodak's Paris office, letterhead emblazoned "Distributors of Kodak Products in Europe and Africa." The body of the fax noted that they had received our order for ten rolls of 16mm film, then added, "We cannot fill the order, however, because we do not know the address of the Kodak office in Nairobi. Please advise."

Jaws dropped. Kodak's Africa distributor didn't know the address of their own office? Had they never shipped film there? Fortunately, Ian's production company in Nairobi had some film stock in the fridge, and he had saved the day by bringing it to Uganda.

After Randy hydrated and got over being crabby, we filmed slow-motion shots of hamlets, people, crops, foliage, and wildlife. I grabbed handheld shots with my Arri from the open side door of a Toyota Hi-Ace van. At first glance, it seemed that each village's open-air market featured piles of reddish rocks. But of course these were yams and other varieties of potatoes, staple foods in this poor country, the median annual income around $300.

On the roads, numerous billboards implored us to "Get Rich From Scrap" at a local metal scrap yard that fed a steel rolling mill. I wondered why the Air France hulk at Entebbe hadn't been torn apart for salvage. Another sign promoted "Designs for Furniture and Executive Coffins."

We had been assigned a "minder" by the Ugandan government, a quiet woman whose job was to accompany us every day and make sure we didn't shoot anything pornographic or violent. Occasionally she was helpful in making arrangements, but mostly she stayed silent in the background and ate our lunch.

Charles Musisi, network manager for the satellite center at Makerere Medical School, showed us around the facility. We had expected an earth station, a large satellite dish and a roomful of equipment, but this installation was quite modest. The antenna on the roof, a small, fixed, unremarkable array, was no larger than my TV aerial at home. The computer gear, two middle-level PC's and a satellite transponder, fit easily on a couple of tables in a small, caged corner of the Library. In those pre-Internet years, this setup allowed 20 minutes of data to be uploaded and downloaded each day as the communication satellite passed overhead.

We had hoped to interview Charles that first day, but our two additional crew people and sound equipment wouldn't arrive until late that afternoon. Our main interview was scheduled for Day Two—with Dr. Ruhakana Rugunda, Uganda's Minister of Works, Transport and Communication.

Since we couldn't shoot sound, Randy asked us to set up for footage of our hosts working in the satellite center. Alan started opening lighting cases, and Rod, our camera assistant, loaded more of Ian's film.

"Oops," I heard from the other room. *Uh oh.*

"The lamps for the lights are in another case," said Alan, "which is still back in Nairobi." The bulbs for our professional lights were expensive and fragile and had been removed and packed securely—and separately—for shipping.

"Sorry, guv'nor," he said. "But they'll be here with my lads on the afternoon plane."

We were dying to shoot something at the med school, so we decided to grab shots of people studying in the Library. None of our lights worked without their bulbs, but most of the students sat near reading lamps. We loaded our fastest film stock and prepared to shoot by lamp light.

As we set up a telephoto shot of a woman engrossed in her books, the power went out in the building, in fact, across the university. Randy was frustrated, but undaunted. Thinking quickly, he scurried around, found some students working near windows, and beckoned us to follow him.

At last we had something to shoot. We framed close-ups of five or six students, absorbed in their reading, some silhouetted, some with a lovely edge of window light on their faces. We took a break after half a roll of film, and Rod called out "Checking the gate!" Part of his normal procedure was to remove the lens from the camera periodically, to inspect where the film passes behind the camera aperture, the "gate" where the film image is exposed. This inspection was critical and only ruined a single frame of film. The worst thing to discover here was a hair or a piece of grit. The camera assistant kept the changing bag and film magazines super-clean to avoid hairs, which looked like huge ropes when the tiny 16mm frames were enlarged many times during projection.

"Uh oh," said Rod. *Bad news?*

"Don't tell me there's a hair in the gate," said Randy.

"No, boss," Rod replied. "It looks like an entire elbow in there." He cleaned the hair, blew out the film chamber with canned air, and we re-shot everything.

We drove to the Ministry to scout Dr. Rugunda's office. He was out at the time, so we planned to film the interview at his desk the next day, with a Ugandan flag in the background. Our government minder woman was quite impressed. Clearly she had never been in such a grand office. Amazingly, in this poor country with such a history of violence, there was little security at this Cabinet-level agency.

Out in the African sun once again, we shot more scenics. Churchill had called Uganda the "pearl of Africa"—the headwaters of the Nile, gorgeous, verdant and lush, nothing like the dry and dusty environment we had anticipated. Despite high humidity and close proximity to the Equator, the 4000-foot elevation around Kampala kept the weather temperate, often 70-75 degrees Fahrenheit. But our visit came at the peak of the fall rainy season. A storm came up late in the day, and Uganda Airlines cancelled the flight from Nairobi with our remaining crew and equipment.

Ian had called around Kampala, and we knew there was nowhere to rent lights or sound gear locally, not even a TV station. Our biggest problem, of course, was the impending interview with the Cabinet minister early the next morning. We couldn't shoot it without sound and lights, and they were still stuck in Nairobi. The next flight would arrive early in the afternoon, but Rugunda was scheduled to leave in mid-morning for a long drive across Uganda to a family affair in his home village.

Mr. F was our client from the company, sent from Tokyo to work with us in Africa and Europe. He was an eager little guy with a face that Randy said "looked like it had been squeezed from a toothpaste tube." He always wore a coat and tie in our travels, regardless of the setting, and he projected an earnestness and loyalty to the company that could verge on the comical. Sometimes we referred to him as Daffy.

Randy and Jane told Daffy the depressing news about our interview. He was upset in a low-key way, sucked in his breath, then groaned, "Ohhh..." which meant "Bummer" in Daffy-speak. He asked about local equipment rental, and Jane explained that was a dead end. Then he ran off to send a fax to his home office.

Randy sometimes likes to shoot from high-rise hotel rooms, for a different perspective on the city and environs. So we decided to film the green hills of Kampala at dusk from the balcony outside Jane's room.

Garbage fires throughout the city gave the scene a surreal look—a hazy cloud lingered over the hills and reddened the ball of the sinking sun.

Randy looked down into the hotel gardens. "Hey, it looks like there's a bunch of bald little Jewish men down there." I followed his gaze. Strutting about on the hotel grounds, I saw a dozen clones of my Uncle Izzie, a pharmacist from Brooklyn I remembered fondly from my youth.

I tilted the camera down, zoomed in, and realized they were huge birds— Marabou storks, also known as Undertaker Birds, nearly five feet tall, carrion birds that loved to feed on small prey, predator kills and carcasses, and rubbish dumps. Many Ugandans duck instinctively when these large scavengers fly overhead. Ominous!

To cheer myself up that evening, I bought a set of Uganda greeting cards at the gift shop in the hotel, with pictures of hippos, elephants, and cranes, each made of tiny strips of wood veneer in black, brown, and tan glued artfully to the plain white card. Each envelope had a tiny person next to a hut, made the same way.

The next morning, we sat glumly at breakfast, dispirited by the fact that we couldn't interview Dr. Rugunda. We could have filmed him outside without lights, but it wouldn't work as a silent picture. Reluctantly, Ian and Jane called the Ministry and cancelled, confirming that he would not be back in town until long after our departure.

Mr. F came bursting in excitedly, waving a fax. "Mr. Randy, Mr. Randy," he called. "The company is very upset about canceling interview. They say you cannot do that."

"Well, Mr. F," Randy told Daffy. "I'm pretty fucking upset, too. But there is no way to shoot an interview without sound. Fax them back and tell them that."

Hours after Rugunda left town, the afternoon flight finally arrived with Steve, our soundman, and Jackie, our lighting assistant, and the rest of our equipment. We headed to Makerere and finally interviewed Charles. This satellite project, put together by Boston-based non-profit SatelLife (aka HealthNet) and supported by our client company, was essential to the university and the medical school.

"This is one case where technology improves the lives of people," Charles told us. "If a doctor here collaborates with a doctor in Mozambique over treatment of burns, they're going to share experience and be more effective in their work.

"It may sound a dream, but it's a reality. Technology really traverses borders. There are no more borders ... With all the developments— stability, peace—we look to a safer world, where people are sharing information, experiences. One global village." Charles' delivery was low key, but heartfelt. At last we had a testimonial from someone on the ground. Our luck was starting to turn.

That's when we met James Tibenderana, a fourth-year medical student from a prominent family who had been exiled in Nigeria during the Amin era. James used the SatelLife-HealthNet system in his work and had strong feelings about its importance. Dissemination of information was vital for the future of his country and all of Africa. He took us to Mulago Hospital and showed us the level of medical care available to the general population.

The wards were filled with beds of sick people, then further cramped by some patients' families, who slept on the floor and cooked for them. It was appalling and sad. I cringed. *What a clean, privileged cocoon we Westerners have created for ourselves, so different from so much of the world.*

James cautioned us not to put anything down on the floor, for fear of collecting germs. I had first heard this type of warning on a shoot years before in a California hospital. At the end of the third day of shooting, as we had coiled up cables and prepared to change floors, a nurse told us, "Be sure to wash your hands before you eat. Hospitals are full of sick people, and this week there's a staph infection going around this place." That night, I fell explosively ill with digestive horrors. The next day, half our crew went down with similar symptoms, some sick for two weeks. And that had taken place in the heart of the squeaky-clean American medical establishment.

We heeded James' warning about the Kampala hospital floors. We filmed him moving among the beds, working with patients, but I couldn't wait to get out of there. Later Rod washed the bottoms of the tripod legs.

Next day, we drove 15-20 kilometers out of Kampala to Kasangati Health Center, where we filmed James conducting a clinic with the local staff. A long parade of patients from the area, mostly moms and babies, sought out immunizations, weighings, or consultation on a variety of outpatient problems. Our film needed these visuals of health care delivery. Ultimately, medicine is about helping people. Technology is just a partner in that effort.

To bounce some general ambient light in the clinic, Alan pointed our 1200-watt HMI light at the ceiling, but the light turned itself off several times as we were shooting. Alan quickly restored it each time, but Jackie, his assistant, never seemed to be around to help.

This was mildly annoying, so I followed the power cable to the back room of the clinic. There was Jackie, sitting next to the light's power ballast, his finger holding down the internal circuit breaker switch. Alan found me and explained that the electricity at the clinic was quite variable, the voltage often much lower than the required 240. So the breaker kept tripping, shutting off the light, a safety feature we had to defeat. The only solution was to force the light to stay on, despite the inadequate and inconsistent voltage, by holding down the breaker.

Later we interviewed James out front under a mango tree, the clinic building and a dozen colorfully dressed women and babies in the background. The SatelLife project, he told us, was "a means by which doctors within Africa and the West can ... exchange ideas, do literature searches ... like a leap from the postal service into the satellite age, whereby we can communicate instantly. This is something which has never happened in Africa." He spoke articulately, with passion and charisma, about the spread of AIDS in Uganda, how he had come back from the relative prosperity of Nigeria to help fight it.

"The future is to think globally, and to act locally. The most exciting thing about living here [in Uganda] is freedom ... The world my children are going to live in will be a peaceful and healthy world."

We cut the camera. After this moving statement, no one spoke for a few seconds, not even Randy. Uganda would be a most memorable sequence in the film. Even Daffy was appeased.

On the road in front of the clinic, a few children carrying burdens on their heads watched as we filmed them. Jane looked down a side road and saw a group of 20 young schoolkids in yellow uniforms walking toward us, perfect imagery to illustrate the future. With the help of our government minder, Jane asked if we could film them. I sat cross-legged in the middle of the dirt road, the camera cradled in my lap, Rod at my side adjusting focus as we shot in slow motion. The kids in yellow came running up the road, laughing, surrounded by greenery. On cue, as they passed the camera, they threw their hands in the air. Visually speaking, Kids = Hope = Future. Especially in slo-mo.

This stunning footage became the opening scene of the whole film, which was titled "A World Together." Before Uganda, we had shot advanced technologies in four other countries, with four more on our itinerary. All were interesting, but none had moved us like this. This film we were making advanced our client company's two idealistic goals for the world, "deepened mutual understanding and the fulfillment of human potential." Improving health care delivery enhanced human potential quite directly! Our world for the past few weeks had seemed like a disjointed progression of airports, hotels, and high-tech locations. Now I could believe it was coming together.

On our last shoot day in Uganda, Ian brought us our film order, which had just arrived from Kodak in Paris. Professional motion picture film is packaged in aluminum film cans, with five 16mm cans fitting in a lightweight carrier, the cardboard about as thick as a cereal box. Our ten-roll order was shipped as two thin carrying boxes taped together with no protection, a shipping label slapped on the side. The package was bashed, dented and misshapen.

We were aghast. Rod took photos to document this woefully inadequate packaging, then he opened it gingerly. Preserving the physical integrity of the camera negative is the most important aspect of the camera assistant's job, from acceptance of raw film stock till delivery of the exposed film to the lab. The film was his temple, and this temple had been defiled. The cans were dented too, which meant the film inside was surely damaged. He took more pictures, then replaced the cans, sadly closed the box, and rejected the shipment with a shudder. Ian sent it back to Kodak, who eventually credited us for the cost of the film and the shipping. Thank goodness Ian had brought his own film for us.

On getaway day, I was up before dawn finishing my packing. At 6, we hopped on the shuttle bus to Entebbe for an 8 a.m. Air Botswana flight to Nairobi.

This time it wasn't dark as we drove past Lake Victoria, the largest lake in Africa and the second largest fresh water lake in the world (after Superior). The sun rose over the water, radiating red, orange, and purple on the clouds above. Surely a new day was dawning for Africa, and the SatelLife project was a significant step in improving lives in Uganda.

At Entebbe, Ian dealt shrewdly with our 16 cases of gear. Since the airline charged by the kilogram for excess baggage, not by case count, he stuck his foot under the luggage scale. The agent called out ridiculously low weights as Rod and I hefted each heavy camera case onto the scale—"Five kilograms ... Nine kilograms"—often less than the weights of the empty cases.

I found it difficult to leave Uganda. This moving story seemed so much more important than software centers, intelligent highways, and translation machines. Years later I learned that the AIDS rate in Uganda peaked around the time we were there and declined later in the 1990s. I often thought about James and wondered how much he had to do with that.

Epilogue: Two months after we left, Ian's production group filmed a short interview for us with Dr. Rugunda when he visited Nairobi. They framed a shot of Rugunda, a physician, sitting with his hands folded in front of a white curtain and a Ugandan flag. Randy asked questions by phone from San Francisco, and the Cabinet minister gave our film an articulate perspective. "After 24 years of turmoil and chaos in the country, Uganda is finally settling down.

"We are focusing on rehabilitation of the infrastructure like roads, all the social services like hospitals and schools, and also on moral rehabilitation, through civic educational programs." The satellite program "helps workers to be better armed to deliver health care services to the population." At last we had his interview.

One January eleven years later, Randy and I traveled to Leeds in the United Kingdom for a medical shoot. I knew James was in London, studying for another advanced degree. We had been in touch by email as I tried to get him copies of "A World Together." On the way back from Leeds, Randy and I stopped in London overnight and the three of us had dinner together.

James met us at our hotel, the Hilton Metropole on Edgware Road, and we walked through the bitter cold to a small Indian restaurant in the neighborhood. It was amazing to see him, many years later and thousands of miles away, as we all bundled up against the London winter so unlike the mild tropical surroundings of our last meeting.

He told us the tide had already turned against HIV in his country before he received his M.D. Uganda took the disease seriously and fought it with a concerted safe-sex campaign, promoting abstinence, monogamy, and condoms. By contrast, neighboring countries like Zimbabwe and South Africa have major AIDS pandemics to this day, mostly through ignorance and denial.

James was in the U.K. earning a Ph.D. from the London School of Hygiene and Tropical Medicine. His concentration was on malaria, which still kills as many as 100,000 people a year in Uganda.

In my work, I usually meet people, get friendly, charm them, gain their confidence, build rapport, invade their space, film their stories ... and never see them again. This was a rare exception. What a pleasure.

At this writing, in the autumn of 2013, Dr. Rugunda serves as Minister of Health for Uganda, after many years in a variety of Cabinet positions and a stint as Uganda's Permanent Representative to the United Nations.

SatelLife is still involved in Uganda, and many other countries. Their focus is now on mobile communications. In a recent seven-year project,

SatelLife helped develop the Uganda Health Information Network project, which supports mobile device-based "health information dissemination, data collection and reporting, and email exchange" for nearly 600 health workers. Because Uganda has "one of the highest burdens of disease in the world but also some of the best cellular telephone coverage in Africa," says SatelLife, "the marriage of handheld technology and cellular telephony represents a watershed moment in the battle against information poverty."

And James Tibenderana, the young medical student we met years ago, has become a respected and frequently published tropical disease expert. He is now Africa Technical Director at the Malaria Consortium in Kampala, which attempts to "improve the prevention, diagnosis and case management of malaria," the leading cause of death in his home country. They distribute malaria drugs and insecticidal mosquito nets, work to prevent malaria during pregnancy, and help develop national guidelines with the Ministry of Health.

Perhaps some day we can return, and Randy won't have to take Lariam.

In Uganda now, James told me in a recent email, "more than 100 mHealth (mobile health) projects aim to use ICT (information and communication technology) to improve the quality of care and expand access to health services. In the film you shot, we had aspirations, and I think technology has made leaps in addressing the hopes we had. Looking back, it is fascinating to have been involved in the process."

I recalled Charles Musisi telling us "there are no more borders," and James saying "the world my children are going to live in will be a peaceful and healthy world."

Thank goodness there are people like Charles, James, and Dr. Rugunda, who are working so hard to make that happen.

See the films "A World Together" and "SatelLife Uganda" online at showdownatshinagawa.com

NYC, PHX, SFO

Dog Years:
Sophie, Pop, and Bill Clinton

I call Mom on my cell phone as I sit tentatively.

"I'm at Bill Clinton's desk in New York, in his chair! We're interviewing him today for *The West Wing Documentary*."

I imagine my tush on the leather seat triggering a Secret Service anti-groupie alarm, armed agents flooding into the former President's office to carry me off. I jump up quickly.

"Tell Pop I'll be there tomorrow. And tell him where I called you from."

A few weeks earlier, our pooch Sophie could barely move from her bed to the rug. When she messed herself, I cried out her name in despair. Embarrassed, she staggered to the back door, slid painfully down the four steps onto her butt on the lawn. Her systems were breaking down.

147

Thirteen was a lot of dog years. The end was near.

She waddled under our deck, toward an open hatch to the crawl space beneath the house. I was afraid she would slip through it and die. I dove into the mud under the deck, grabbed her rear legs, and pulled our 90-pound mutt out as gently as I could. I replaced the hatch cover, and Sophie ran to the other end of the mucky world under the deck, far from my reach. She stayed there for hours.

Next day, I got a funny feeling and went to check on her. She lay still on her bed, the light gone from her eyes. The grandfather clock in the living room struck noon, reminding me of my dad, who had built it for us ten years before. Now he was immobilized in a Phoenix hospital after a massive stroke, and Sophie was dead. I sobbed as I compulsively washed her food and water bowls and rolled up her bed.

Clinton loved being President and tells us he ended his tenure in the White House more idealistic than when he started. Asked about future plans, he mentions casually that both he and strategist James Carville are apparently eligible to run for President of France. Because Carville and Clinton were born in Louisiana and Arkansas, respectively, both parts of the formerly French Louisiana Purchase, they could hypothetically move to France, establish residency, and run for office. "I don't think I will," says Clinton, with a broad smile. "I'm sure I would soon start to take flak for my French accent."

Our talk is his first major television interview since leaving office, and he sticks around for pictures and chat afterward. His dog died recently and I want to bring that up, but the woman who catered our shoot has a lot to say to him about Bush, and I'm too starstruck to break in.

The day after meeting Clinton in New York, I visit Pop in a rehab facility in Scottsdale, only a mile from where he and Mom live. My dad has always been a Renaissance man—musician, teacher, and author of over thirty books on crafts, hobbies, and the outdoors, a tough old bird who could build or do anything. He's a smart, accomplished, multifaceted guy. I've always been different—more one-sided, focused on my career as a cameraman.

Nearly 90—about the same dog age as Sophie—the man who could do everything now lies helpless in bed at a nursing home, fed by a tube, his eyesight and hearing impaired, paralyzed on one side and incontinent. During our visit, I describe shooting *The West Wing Documentary*. "We interviewed Bill Clinton yesterday in New York," I tell him, "and tomorrow we'll meet Gerald Ford in Palm Springs."

"They named a theatre after him," he replies, with a twinkle.

"You mean Ford's Theatre, where Lincoln was shot?" I laugh. He grins, happy that I've gotten his corny joke. He's always been a force of nature, and somehow, we still fully expect him to recover.

Dear President Clinton:

I met you last week. I was the cameraman, the tall guy behind the director during the interview you did for The West Wing *in your office ...*

As a former government major and White House buff, I thoroughly enjoyed shooting The West Wing Documentary Special *and meeting so many seminal political figures of the past several decades, including, besides yourself, Presidents Carter and Ford, and Secretary Kissinger.*

You and I are the same age and same class in school, and ... I had imagined that, if we met, we might discuss political sentiments, the issue-of-the-day.

However, what was in my heart the day we transformed your lovely office into a little studio was wishing to offer my condolences on the death of your dog Buddy. My family recently went through the same kind of loss. Our pooch Sophie died in March at age thirteen, and life has changed since then. The house feels very empty without her ... She was big and black, a boxer-lab mix, scary-looking but meek as a lamb, and great with kids.

My wife and I always walked Sophie to school with our two sons ... For years, children we didn't know would come up to us on the street, greet Sophie by name, and exchange a scratch behind the ears for a wetdown. She had a prodigious tongue and a thick whiplike tail. Together they made for an intense licking and wagging experience, especially when she was happy, which was most of the time.

After she died, we scattered Sophie's ashes at sunset at the dog park on San Francisco Bay where she spent many happy hours. Then we spent the evening digging through old photos and movies of our family growing up with her. Laughing and spending time together helped us heal the hurt of losing her.

That's what I wish I had told you at the time we met, but being busy and tongue-tied prevented my saying all that. In any case, I hope you are able to have some peace about losing Buddy. Remember the good times and the wonderful, unconditional love that only dogs and precious few humans practice regularly ...

If you do run for President of France, I wish you the best of luck. You can always work on your French accent.

With best wishes,

Bill Zarchy

I don't expect Clinton to respond, but writing to him about Sophie is cathartic.

Two days before *The West Wing Documentary* airs on NBC, Pop passes away. I watch the show with my family and some close friends. Shooting this network primetime special has been a great opportunity for me, and I burst into tears during the opening music as I see my credit over an aerial shot of the White House. Pop didn't get to see my show, but at least I got to tell him about it.

Four months later, to my amazement, I receive a letter with an embossed, gold presidential seal and William Jefferson Clinton printed at the top.

Dear Bill:

Thank you for the kind letter you sent to me after the filming of The West Wing *Documentary. I was so touched by it and regret that I was unable to respond sooner.*

I was sorry to learn about the loss of your dog Sophie. While our family has a new puppy now, I still miss Buddy very much. He will always hold a special place in my heart, which, as a fellow dog lover, I know you will understand.

It was a great pleasure for me to participate in The West Wing *special episode, and I'm grateful for all you did to make it such a success. I'm glad you took the time to write and send you my best wishes,*

Sincerely,

Bill Clinton

So much has happened since my letter to him. *The West Wing Documentary Special* has won an Emmy Award as Outstanding Special Class Program, defeating, among others, an *I Love Lucy Special* and *Survivor*. Since Pop's death, in a profound way, I have reevaluated who I am and my place in the world, diversifying my interests and activities. New doors have opened up for me in teaching and writing.

After Pop died, a friend told me that, since his own father's passing, he had found more and more of his dad in himself. "So in a way, you have *more* of your dad to look forward to, not less." Indeed, I keep finding more and more of Pop in myself, my work, relationships, and personality. He is a part of me in ways I'm just beginning to understand.

And when I showed my cousin a recent picture of me with my family, she said, "Oh Billy, you look just like your father!" It seems I have more of my dad to look *like*, too.

Pop lived in another city. Though we were close, we only talked or emailed every couple of weeks. Sophie was my pal, constant companion, and family roommate, hanging out with us all over the house, offering love without judgment at any time, and expecting only affection and kibble in return. Losing her has ached on a daily basis.

Time has passed since the emotional roller coaster of losing my dad and my dog, during a career highpoint filming presidents. *The West Wing* is off the air, but I still cry at the opening music when I watch an episode on DVD. Like the Clintons, we've gotten a new puppy, a cute, rescued mutt named Montana. Abused or abandoned at an early age, she is timid and a bit neurotic—the opposite of her predecessor. But we lavish her with unconditional love. That's how we keep Sophie in our hearts.

See video from "The West Wing Documentary" at showdownatshinagawa.com

WILLIAM JEFFERSON CLINTON

September 3, 2002

Bill Zarchy
Director of Photography

Dear Bill:

Thank you for the kind letter you sent to me
after the filming of the West Wing documentary. I was so touched by it and regret
that I was unable to respond sooner.

I was sorry to learn about the loss of your
dog Sophie. While our family has a new
puppy now, I still miss Buddy very much.
He will always hold a special place in my
heart, which, as a fellow dog lover, I know
you understand.

It was a great pleasure for me to participate in the West Wing special episode, and
I'm grateful for all you did to make it such
a success. I'm glad you took the time to
write and send you my best wishes.

Sincerely,

Bill Clinton

The Big Break:
Malaise in Manila

The day we visited Subic Bay to look for locations, it was locked up tight.

"We can't get in, Boss!" Romy told me.

"What's wrong?"

"Well, they can't find the key. The last Americans left three months ago, and it seems like no one has gone inside the base since then."

Officials from the Philippine national government and the City of Olongapo passed the buck. No one knew how to get into the former U.S Naval Base. At last an official in the mayor's office discovered keys to some of the buildings.

We opened one small warehouse with shabby offices in the front and a shop area in the back. The shop had a metal rollup door, which didn't quite reach the ground. The power was off at first, and we explored in the semi-dark and walked through what I thought was a pile of dried leaves. With more light, I realized with a groan that the two-inch-long brown ribbed things crunching under my feet were not plant matter.

"Ooh, what are these?" I asked.

"Hey, what do you think, Direc? Take a look."

"They've got little legs!"

Cockroaches. Dead ones that had blown in under the door.

Romy started to laugh. I was visiting the Philippines to direct an action movie for a Japanese company. In one scene, a man was supposed to eat a cockroach, a live one. When I had first arrived and asked Romy and Archie how we would find an actor who would eat a cockroach, they had laughed then too.

"No problem, Boss." Apparently lots of actors eat roaches in movies in the Philippines.

I was pleased. Our locations were working out and cockroach eaters abounded. This movie was the Big Break I had been waiting for, and things were going well.

Kurosawa Wants You

A few weeks earlier, John McD had called me from Tokyo: "Mr. Kurosawa would like you to direct *Emerald Knight*. Can you come to Japan next week to meet with us and then travel on to Manila to scout locations?"

Can I?

You bet! A filmmaker's wet dream.

Except ... I already knew he wasn't Akira Kurosawa, legendary director of classic films like *Seven Samurai*, but a Japanese TV-movie producer with the same last name, now executive producer of an international sci-fi action-adventure movie, scheduled to be shot in the Philippines.

Never underestimate the power of advertising. John had first called me in response to my Director listing in *The Reel Directory*, northern California's media guidebook. I did direct a bit, but nearly all of my work was as director of photography, head of the camera crew. *The Reel Directory* listed me in both categories.

I was surprised when I met with John McD to discuss his intriguing project. He didn't look Irish. Though his dad was Irish-American, John's mom was Japanese, and he had grown up on both sides of the Big Pond. Most recently, John had been living in San Francisco, translating, studying film, and guiding foreign film crews around the States.

When he and his wife planned to move back to Tokyo, his old pal Kurosawa, a producer of seven or eight Japanese TV movies, had offered him the job of field producer for *Emerald Knight* and had asked him to help find a director, a native English speaker, for his first English-language picture.

I was fluent in English—born in Brooklyn and raised on Long Island— but light in feature film experience. I certainly had never directed a movie before!

Nevertheless, we enjoyed talking for a couple of hours. Sure I'd never see him again, I sent him off to Tokyo with my latest demo reel and a copy of a one-hour music video I'd shot with rap artist MC Hammer.

So I was stunned when he called a few weeks later to offer the job. *Why me?*

"Are you sure?" I asked incredulously.

"Yes," he said. "Mr. Kurosawa was very impressed with your work on the MC Hammer film."

I thought for a moment. The Hammer video, shot during the height of his popularity in the early 90s, had featured dramatic dialogue scenes and five songs, all carefully choreographed and filmed in 35mm with multiple cameras on dollies, cranes, and Steadicam. It had won a Grammy award and was an impressive piece of work, but I had been the director of photography, not the director. *Does shooting Hammer dancing hip-hop with his posse in the streets of Oakland qualify me to direct a futuristic drama in the Philippines?*

Apparently Kurosawa thought it did. I asked for a day to think it over. *Do I want to do this? Is this a flaky deal that will end in disaster, or a genuine opportunity to jump into the movie business abroad?*

I was hungry to work on movies, but had never wanted to move to Hollywood. Too much traffic and smog and phony hype, compared to the mellower lifestyle in San Francisco, where I mostly shot high-end corporate projects for Silicon Valley and a smattering of commercials and musical performance.

I enjoyed my work and the wonderfully inventive and creative people I worked with, but I never made a ton of dough. Occasionally I got a particularly challenging project like the MC Hammer film, with a large crew. I had managed to keep my creative juices flowing, but I did have a hankering to do national work. Or international work.

John's project was outside my usual comfort zone, but I had to consider: *Is* Emerald Knight *my Big Break, the next step in my journey, catapulting me into an international film career? Is this the first of many, or even just several?* I fantasized crisscrossing the Pacific on filming trips, then jetting off to glittery film premieres in Japan and Hong Kong with my family in tow.

What do I have to lose? We were coming out of a recession. As my wife Susan pointed out sagely, no one else was clamoring for my services just then—her polite way of saying, "So, what else have you got to do?"

I called John back the next day and agreed to direct the film, but with four conditions:

(1) *Miles*—All my air travel must be on United. Even then I was a mileage

whore.

(2) *Cash*—I must be paid weekly, in cash, in U.S. dollars. If the project fell apart, I wouldn't lose more than a week's pay.

(3) *Privacy*—I must always have my own room. A few months before, I had worked with a Japanese crew in the States who thought that five guys bunking in an RV constituted adequate accommodations.

(4) *Points*—I wanted a percentage of the profit of the film.

Kurosawa, through John, approved my conditions. After a brief negotiation, we agreed that I would direct the shooting of *Emerald Knight* for $2,200 per week and supervise the editing for $1,500. This was much less than I wanted, but more than they had budgeted. Even if it wasn't my Big Break, what else did I have to do?

Emerald (K)night

I planned to leave for Japan ten days after that first call with John, on the date of Bill Clinton's inauguration, January 20, 1993. *Bummer! I'll miss the swearing-in.* I was eager to see a Democrat move into the White House, but I was now the director of an international action movie, and Clinton would just have to wait. I had a lot to do before I could leave the country.

No one had email then, and the Internet was just a dream. International long distance was expensive, but John and I spoke on the phone nearly every day, and he sent me faxes, in care of my local copy shop. When a printed version of the script arrived by air express, I was ready to roll. Finally, I'd see what this film was about.

Emerald Knight was set in a seedy metropolis in the "not-too-distant future." The hero, Dirk Nelson, was an agent of Concorp, a consortium of oppressive corporations with broad, worldwide police powers. He decided to go undercover among the Walkers, the ordinary citizens, to investigate a series of bombings. In the course of the story, he fell in love with Vel, a beautiful woman who—of course—turned out to be the leader of the resistance, known as Emerald Night. All this took place in a depressing and dreary world with obscenely polluted air and no plants. The air was so bad that plants couldn't survive, and most people moved about in underground tunnels.

I had questions.

"A world without plants? Why are we shooting in the Philippines? It's a tropical country! And why is the title *Emerald Knight*, with a K, but the rebel group is Emerald Night, without? Does the K stand for Kurosawa?"

Not surprisingly, the choice to film in the Philippines had been economic. The Philippine military had offered Mr. Kurosawa logistical help with the movie at an attractive price, including personnel, vehicles, aircraft, and weapons. He was certain we would find rundown locations in Manila and at the former U.S. Naval Base at Subic Bay that would lend themselves to our story. The title, with the "K," was supposed to be a playful pun: Dirk ends up becoming a knight, a hero of the resistance.

Playful, or confusing and annoying? I held my tongue. I began to think of the title as *Emerald (K)night*, with the "K" in mental parentheses. *Playfully.*

Despite the fact that I had just been hired, the main stars of *Emerald Knight* had been cast for some time. Monika Schnarre, a Canadian supermodel who had appeared in one film, would play Vel. And Dick Fly, a Dutch fighter who was popular in Japan, had been hired to play the part of Dirk Nelson. He had never acted before.

"Dick Fly? Is that really his name? Can he act? Does he even speak English?"

"I'll find out," said John. I was less worried about Monika, who was a native English speaker and would at least look good on screen.

John discovered that Dick Fly did speak English. "He's been compared to

159

Jean-Claude Van Damme," the Belgian-born martial artist and film star. *By whom*, I wondered?

I plunged into research, renting several Van Damme movies. I was impressed. The Belgian was muscular and attractive, yet vulnerable. Cute, with a twinkle in his eye. And he was quite a fighter, his shirt often in tatters around his torso. At least once in each film, he appeared completely nude, viewed from behind. Nice derriere, I thought.

Check Dick's butt, I muttered to myself, as I wondered how in the world I would do that.

I also watched Monika's movie, *Waxwork II: Lost in Time.* She was attractive, tall, with full lips and a square jaw. I couldn't tell much about her acting from her portrayal of Sarah Brightman, hampered by dialogue like this: "Vell perhaps if you spent less time vith that heap of brain-damaged flesh in the basement and more time vith me, I vouldn't have to seek pleasures elsevere! Vould I?"

As the departure date drew closer, my friends started ragging me about my new project. "Dick Fly? Are you serious?" said Randy. "Doesn't it seem just a little, uh, flaky?"

Totally. Compared with my usual work in the commercial and corporate film worlds—generous budgets, safe concepts, good pay—*Emerald Knight* was a trip to Jupiter. Other than John, who was half-Japanese and a dual citizen, I was the only American involved so far.

A Filipino-American friend who spoke Tagalog wanted me to bring him along as my assistant. I couldn't. "Just don't ride in any helicopters over there," he warned. A crew guy from the Bay Area had recently been killed in a chopper accident during a shoot in the Philippines. I shuddered as I thought of the aerial shots planned for parts of our film.

My excitement mounted. Other than a shoot in Munich a few months before, I had not filmed outside the U.S. since the 70s, when I had visited Japan twice and all around the Pacific Rim. I'd never been to the

Philippines. I knew I'd be cramming my oversized body into small airline seats for many hours in the near future, but it didn't matter.

I can survive the plane flights, I told myself, pushing down the urge to panic, *and I can direct this movie.*

Mercifully, my departure was pushed back one day. I got to watch the Clinton inauguration after all, then hopped on a United nonstop to Japan the next day.

Bring on Dick Fly. I'm ready!

Arrival in Tokyo

John and Kurosawa met me at Narita Airport. Kurosawa looked younger than I had imagined, prosperous in a long leather coat. We retrieved my bags and piled into his Maserati. It was cold, and a freezing rain had recently passed through.

Suddenly, after an eleven-hour flight from San Francisco, I was sitting in an Italian car (steering wheel on the left, same as in the States) in a country where people drove on the left side of the road, like the Brits. Everything felt backwards. I was on the wrong side of the car on the wrong side of the slushy streets. Kurosawa beamed a big, confident smile. He drove with his left hand, his right arm thrown casually up on the seat back next to him, as I lurched around in the passenger seat. My normal senses of balance and correct road position were reversed and distorted by my jetlagged perceptions. It seemed that my host was missing barriers and other cars by mere inches.

He asked me something about Yokohama, but I didn't catch his meaning. John explained from the backseat that we were having dinner there with our male lead, who had just flown in from Holland for a fight.

Dick Fly was part of the Rings fighting circuit, featured on Japanese cable channel Wowow. We met with him and several of his Dutch teammates at their hotel in Yokohama. The publicist, a Japanese lady, guided us toward an Italian restaurant in the lobby. But I didn't want spaghetti on my first visit to Japan in 15 years! She relented and whisked us up the elevator to a warmly lit room with tatami mats, tempura, sushi, and sashimi.

Of course it was much more expensive, but I was the director. *It's good to be the king.*

Dick and I shook hands when we met. He was over six feet tall, 250 lbs. of solid muscle. High cheekbones on a muscular skull, a one-inch fringe of red hair on top, shaved on the sides. Downright grim at first. No smile upon meeting, none of Van Damme's charm or cuteness or twinkle. I was disappointed and couldn't imagine how this low charisma level would translate to the big screen. He was the hero and needed the audience to like him. I resisted the urge to check out Dick's butt.

But then he smiled, and his expression softened. He looked like a little boy, though a very large and buff little boy. Blue eyes, now with a hint of amusement. I started to feel a little better. *Okay*, I thought, *I can work with that.* He did speak English, but very quietly, and with a Dutch accent. He and the others spoke often about their "doh-yo," and it was a while before I realized they meant *dojo*—their training center.

After dinner, I looked forward to some rest. Adrenaline could only take me so far.

But I was excited to be back in Japan, so I started channel surfing in my room. Many stations featured recaps of sumo wrestling matches, which fascinated me, and repetitive interviews with one odd-looking wrestler. He spoke Japanese, wore traditional sumo robes and hair, but his dark skin and features were not Japanese. *Who is he?* The "bilingual" button on the TV remote brought no English explanation. From the replays, he had clearly dominated the tournament, and he was HUGE!

Akebono

At breakfast, I saw in the papers that a powerful sumo wrestler named

Akebono had been granted the title of *Yokozuna*, the first Grand Champion in a number of years.

Hawaiian/African-American, his name was Chad Rowan, he was over six-feet-eight, and he weighed nearly 500 lbs! Akebono meant "sunrise" in Japanese, one of a few dozen sumo names that have been recycled several times in the three-hundred-year recorded history of the sport. I wondered how he got along in Japanese culture, where I often felt monstrous at six-feet-four.

An article in *Time* magazine probed "The Clinton Style," as the international press tried to figure out our new leader. An avid jogger, Clinton wore a Timex Ironman Triathlon digital watch, not a typically pricey bauble like a Rolex. I wore one too. I already felt an affinity with the new Pres. We were both early Baby Boomers (born within a year of each other), both went to Ivy League schools, both skirted Vietnam. And we had an old friend in common.

But knowing that we share a preference for the same $40 watch makes me swell with pride, or kvell, as my grandmother would say.

John and Kurosawa presented me with business cards and a bound copy of the script. We attended a production meeting at the office of the distribution company that was putting up the money. My electric shaver had died, so I went unshaven. I met Mr. H, the head of the company; Toshi, a Japanese director of photography who was slated to shoot our film; and Jun, an assistant director who would keep us organized. They were all sharply dressed, and I felt stubbly and shabby. I hoped they would consider me a wacky American artist, not a grubby, gargantuan *gai-jin*.

To compensate, I tried to charm them. I was accustomed to using humor to relax my crews, a technique that had worked in other settings. I teased Jun: "In the States, the assistant director does all the work and the director takes all the credit. Is it the same way here?" He looked uncomfortable answering. Some of those at the meeting laughed nervously, but mostly I amused myself, as my attempt at being funny fizzled in translation.

Toshi had recently shot a feature film called *Tokyo Decadence,* and I made a note to check it out. I had brought a book of *Film Terms in Japanese,* which intrigued my new friends, until they realized it translated only from English to Japanese. Some of the entries were real industry lingo, they told me, but some were laughable (and inaccurate) literal translations. I also impressed them with my Timex Ironman Triathlon digital watch and explained my close connection with Bill Clinton.

They brought in an actor named Watanabe and asked if we could cast him as Toda, the villain in the film. He spoke a little English, but of course I had no idea if he could act. Through John, Kurosawa told me that Watanabe was a big box office attraction in Japan, so I agreed. And thus we cast the president of Concorp.

John and I met with Brian, the scriptwriter, an American expatriate and magazine editor living in Tokyo, at his apartment in the Meguro district. He told us of the early days of the film: "I was asked by Kurosawa to write a letter in English to Dick Fly (or his agent), asking him to be in a movie."

Brian: "What kind of movie?"

Kurosawa: "What kind of movie would be good?"

Brian: "You mean you don't have a script?"

Kurosawa: "Yes, we do." (Which I found out later meant 'No, we don't.')

So Brian had written one. We spent hours going through his screenplay, trying to eliminate contradictions and smooth out transitions. Eventually, we ordered a clam-and-squid pizza from Domino's and settled back to watch Dick Fly and the others from his "doh-yo" on Wowow.

The Rings fighting circuit was a precursor to Ultimate Fighting and other mixed martial arts that became popular in the U.S. years later. It was like kickboxing, but with fewer obvious rules. They punched and they kicked and they threw each other around the ring. The matches seemed pretty real, unlike American wrestling.

Dick Fly had an impressive build. Broad muscled shoulders, v-shaped torso, slabs of muscle everywhere. As the referee drew both fighters close for a quick inspection before the bout began, Dick flexed his pectorals rhythmically, first both together, then alternately. He fought fiercely and won two of his three matches. He kneed opponents in the skull, threw them to the ground, kicked viciously, pounded with pile driver fists. He was powerful and agile and quick and not above taunting his opponents with a mischievous grin. He never showed that little-boy smile again, but this was a tough-guy setting.

"Some of those moves will work in his role as Dirk," I told John and Brian.

After Rings, we rented and screened *Tokyo Decadence*, Toshi's main feature film credit, a hard-to-watch story of a prostitute locked up and tortured in a hotel room. I could tell, despite not understanding the Japanese dialogue, that Toshi could do dramatic lighting—lots of backlight and shadow—and that encouraged me.

Brian's girlfriend Yumiko and John's wife Takako joined us, and we spent the evening club-hopping in the Roppongi district. One glittery nightclub we visited had a 50s band theme. Another was all Beatles, all the time, where they greeted "Mr. Brian" and brought out a Scotch bottle with his name on it and a liquid level scribed in white marker from his last visit. Brian explained (with "Love, Love Me Do" blasting in the background) that "buying a bottle is much cheaper here than buying individual drinks." Looking around at the elegantly turned-out young crowd around me, once again I felt underdressed.

1st Trip to Manila

We flew to Manila to meet our Filipino staff and scout locations for a few days. At our hotel, I looked around and absorbed the ambience.

In a few days I had gone from cold, rainy San Francisco to freezing, slushy

Tokyo. Now I was in the tropics for the first time in years. I sat back in the refrigerated lobby air, a relief from the hot, dank, smoggy streets we had driven through. I enjoyed the view of lush greenery. *But how will we ever be able to create a world without plants in this environment?*

We met Archie, our local production manager, ruggedly handsome and an actor himself. His assistant Romy was shorter, a bit rounder, and quite gregarious.

They peppered me with questions: "How do you want to shoot this fight scene? What kinds of locations do you want? How about props, costumes, armaments, vehicles, special effects? What other movies have you directed? What are our stars like? Can we really shoot *Emerald Knight* in four weeks?"

The only thing I know for sure, I thought, is that we need more time to shoot.

Everyone called our hotel the Ramada—pronouncing it *RAH-mah-dah*—but the signs all claimed that the place was named the Manila Midtown Hotel. The Midtown hadn't been part of the Ramada chain for 15 years, as it turned out, but was still known by its old name. The Ramada was 21 stories tall, with a good gym, nice rooms, and a posted "watcher" on every floor to discourage thieves. This employee, a uniformed young man or woman, would stand up at a podium near the elevators all day (or all night), greet guests, and log room numbers, comings and goings.

Metro Manila experienced near-daily, unpredictable, rolling electrical blackouts lasting four to six hours. Archie assured me we would always have generators for filming. During blackouts at the Ramada, the hotel's emergency generator powered only one elevator and one hanging lamp in each guestroom. If the electricity went off during the night, we had no hot water for showers in the morning.

Aging power plants bore responsibility for this unstable situation. Plants built mostly during the fifty years of American rule in the first half of the twentieth century frequently went offline for repairs and maintenance. My Filipino friends explained the repairs were just Band-Aids—serious surgery was needed. The problem, of course, was money.

We scouted locations in a ten-passenger Toyota Hi-Ace van. Manila traffic was ferocious and smelly and slow. Besides cars and stinky diesel trucks and buses, we were constantly buzzed by swarms of small motorized bikes of all kinds, some jammed with families of five or six. Jeepneys provided the predominant public transport—small, open jitney buses, with crowded bench seating for ten or twelve and easy access and egress. Jeepneys, originally kluged together from old Willys Jeep fronts and parts left behind by the U.S. military, were now manufactured as jitneys and sported colorful, bright, unique paint jobs.

 Crushing poverty surrounded us. Shantytowns abounded, many built from corrugated aluminum or other crude shed materials, tucked in among the huge office buildings and high-rise hotels and apartments of downtown Manila, in and around the warehouse districts and middle-class neighborhoods. Every restaurant, club, and hotel employed an armed guard at the entrance, usually some young guy in a dark blue uniform with a pistol on his belt. Pitiful people begged at smoky freeway entrances or sold roses or papers in noxious highway tunnels. Kidnapping for ransom was in the news, particularly of wealthy Chinese residents.

We stopped at a corner, and I heard Archie make loud kissing sounds with his lips to call a newspaper boy. He beckoned the guy over with his fingers down, a politeness in many cultures. Later he told me it would be rude to summon a person by whistling or beckoning with fingers up.

"Only a dog should be called that way," he said.

Comelec

One of our most interesting locations in Manila was in the walled city of Intramuros (Spanish for "inside the walls")—the ruins of the old Comelec building, the Commission on Elections, which had been bombed during World War II, when most of downtown Manila was destroyed. Also known as the Aduana from its time as a customs hall, this ruin was located between busy streets and open to the sky, with few windows or openings on the lower floors. Once inside, you were in a different place and time. Comelec had five levels of staircases, hallways, and stone and concrete construction, with little interior design or decoration remaining. The bare corridor walls were cave-like and decrepit, much like the tunnels in our story. And there were no plants.

As we wandered through, a production assistant named Gene, a little guy, followed us and videotaped various corners and angles. His job, like PAs everywhere, was to do whatever needed doing.

The Comelec building had been used as a location many times before. We could avoid the noise of the traffic outside by dubbing the sound later, which would be necessary with any scenes shot in busy parts of the city. We would shoot at night during the dry season, so sun or rain coming through the roof wouldn't ruin the mood or cause trouble.

During our scout, we watched a local film crew building a prison set in one corner of this huge edifice. Gene and Archie chatted with them in Tagalog. A new Roger Corman-produced thriller was scheduled to shoot prison scenes in a few weeks.

At last I was starting to see the film in my mind: *We can stage several scenes in this bombed-out ruin. We'll fabricate a street market for various encounters between Dirk and the common people, stage dialogue at a food stall around the corner, and light mysterious intrigues in moody, shadowy, yet electrifying ways.*

I had recently seen Ridley Scott's *Blade Runner* again. Comelec—and Brian's script—evoked similar imagery. Even the ultra-modern offices of the evil Concorp would have a seedy look.

I tried to imagine Dick Fly, his shirt in tatters around his torso, in a fight to the death on the steps of the Comelec Building, and my cameraman's mind started to catalogue the shots we would need to cover the action.

But wait, besides the visuals, I'm the director here, and I've got actors to direct and a story to tell, not just pictures to make. For the thousandth time I wondered: *Can these people act?* If this was my Big Break, I needed them to act.

At each pause in our meandering, Jun would ask questions, mutter to John, and make notes in Japanese. English would be the only common language on our production, and I was concerned about my ability to communicate with everyone. *Thank goodness John is here to translate.*

We visited the former provincial capitol building at Pasig about an hour outside Manila, a sprawling stone ruin. This mansion still held interior fixtures, pieces of tiled flooring, plaster walls, and ornate ceilings intact in some places, ripped back to the lath and stone in others. One bathroom still had shower and toilet fixtures that squatters had used, despite the fact that there was no running water. Fireplaces with carved wooden mantles, half-ruined by sun and rain, stood in grand rooms next to gaping holes in the floor, debris everywhere. Gene glided about with his video camera, Jun made notes, and Kurosawa beamed at this fine location and chatted quietly with Archie and Romy about business arrangements.

We decided to use Pasig as the Emerald Night hideout, detention room, and guard-house locations. All these could be staged in upper rooms or courtyards where there was little or no greenery, if we restricted our view to certain angles.

It had been a long day. Back at the Ramada, I stared at a card in my room that proclaimed: "Our skillful and attractive masseuses provide relaxing, therapeutic massage, in our studio or in the privacy of your own room. Swedish or Shiatsu."

I could use a massage, I thought, *but it's too late now. Skillful and attractive?*

Ermita and Mabini

One of our locations in an office building in the Ermita district turned out to be near a new McDonald's, at that time a novelty in Manila. We stopped in for Egg McMuffins with hash browns. We sought to rent a vacant office, to build a grubby futuristic set for Dirk's command post. As I stood in that office and conferred about the set with John and Kurosawa and Jeffrey, our art director, I looked outside.

"Look at the view!"

"So?"

"The tall buildings of the skyline are wrapped in thick smog."

"Yes, I'm sorry, Direc."

"Don't be. It looks perfect!"

In many ways, Manila is the seedy, dystopic society in the movie. Except for all these damn plants!

Outside and across the street was a vacant dirt lot used for parking. We needed a series of "holevator" shots, where Dirk emerged from and returned to the underground tunnels the Concorp people used for travel. Archie and Romy suggested renting the lot, digging a huge hole, and building the holevator set there. We also planned to use a tall office building nearby as the exterior of Concorp headquarters.

I soon realized that our local staff preferred this neighborhood because of its proximity to the Mickey D's. We ate under the golden arches whenever we were in Ermita—breakfast, lunch, or dinner. Other times we chowed down on *sashimi* and *tempura* at the ubiquitous Japanese restaurants all around Manila. Other than fresh seafood, McDonald's was the only non-Japanese food that Kurosawa would eat.

Occasionally, when we were out without Mr. K, Archie or Romy would take us for Philippine food, and I saw what I had been missing: lumpia, a kind of fried eggroll, and all sorts of rice dishes with combinations like chicken and shrimp, or pork and fish, with vegetables.

We also liked to eat at a huge seafood restaurant on Mabini Street, filled with families and lined with refrigerated display cases showing all kinds of fish on ice. Mr. K and the others would wander from case to case, choosing this fish or that, specifying cooking instructions. We would share all this food, along with vast quantities of bottled San Miguel beer, brewed just a few miles away. Here my companions taught me the Filipino toast *Mabuhay* ("Hooray!"), the Japanese toast *Kanpai* ("Complete defeat!"), and the Japanese custom of pouring beer for your friends, then letting them pour for you. No matter whatever else happened, I thought, this was a rich multicultural experience!

We searched for a location to use as the Hideaway Nightclub—the place where Dirk and Vel meet, and the secret headquarters of the Emerald Night resistance. We checked out a German bar on del Pilar Avenue called the Fischfang, which served a mean *Wienerschnitzel* and was filled with aquariums and unique stone walls. *Could a world without plants have lots of tropical fish? Why not?*

But the place was too small to shoot in, and they stayed open 24 hours a day. We favored instead the Remember When Nostalgia Bar, a larger place we could decorate, nestled amongst eating places and the ever-present strip clubs on Mabini, where topless girls jiggled their booties unenthusiastically on stages in view of the street.

Back to Tokyo

After a week or so, I was scheduled to return to Tokyo with Kurosawa and John, and then home. Jun stayed in Manila to keep working on arrangements for our shoot coming up in March, in about six weeks. As we walked through Ninoy Aquino International Airport in Manila, we saw dozens of grim young Filipino men in matching new denim shirts and pants waiting in line. People were among the Philippines' biggest exports. Seeing these overseas workers on their way out of the country brought home the reality of most poor countries—many people can earn more money abroad than at home.

Four hours later, we entered the vast customs hallway at Narita in Tokyo and noticed uncharacteristically long lines at the inspection tables.

"This never happens," muttered Kurosawa, and soon we saw the reason why: a video crew was shooting customs officers opening suitcases. After a long wait, it was my turn, and they searched every inch of my belongings, trying to look industrious for the camera. As a customs agent with big teeth and a crooked smile examined my dirty underwear, he looked up at me, stared into my eyes and said very slowly, "Do you smoke mah-ree-wah-nah?"

"No, no, of course not," I sputtered, aghast. *Does anyone ever say yes?*

"Hah-sheesh?" he pressed. "You smoke hah-sheesh?"

"No, no. No hashish." He looked at me sharply. I resisted the urge to be a wise guy, and he let me enter Japan for an overnight layover.

Next day, one of Mr. K's office workers came to my hotel, handed me an envelope with 22 crisp $100 bills, and advised me that my flight to San Francisco had been cancelled. I had already checked out of my room, so we took the shuttle bus to the airport terminal, where United was able to book me on another nonstop four hours later. I settled down with my book in the departure lounge.

The place was abuzz. The sumo master Akebono, the toast of Japan, had come through there on his way to Hawaii just a few minutes before. I sat in the waiting room and overheard an American describe the wrestler to his wife.

"My God, honey, what a big boy! I don't know how he can fit in the airline seats. Maybe he gets two. And what about the toilet on the plane? How does he use it?"

I refuse to contemplate the bathroom logistics of a 500-pounder who towers over me. Truly he must feel gigantic in Japan. An airport safety video in the terminal showed greasy white guys with ponytails and black guys with scarred faces snatching purses from naïve Japanese tourists in American cities. Eventually, I got to fly home.

Faxing from Home

I immediately bought and installed a fax machine, finally entering the twentieth century. Over the next few weeks, John and I burned up the wires between my living room and his office in Japan. Every night I would get up in the wee hours and excitedly check my fax to see the latest pages sent at the end of the Tokyo workday.

"It's magic," I burbled excitedly to my kids. "It's an instantaneous miracle. John is 5,000 miles away, feeding those pages into his machine over there, seconds before I catch them spilling out of our machine over here."

"How do the pages get here, Daddy?" asked my son Razi. "Do they teleport?"

We exchanged hundreds of pages of costume design sketches, location lists, script breakdowns, brochures for interesting-looking household items from Japan that could be aged and altered to look like future technology, lists of crew we were bringing from Japan and crew we were hiring in Manila, travel itineraries, and drafts of a letter of agreement between me and Paradise Entertainment, Kurosawa's company.

Monika Schnarre, who had been cast to play the female lead, called me from L.A. to chat about the film. Her agent had made the deal, and she had never met Mr. K. She offered to fly to the Bay Area for a quick meet-and-greet. We set a date.

John faxed a question from Kurosawa: would I be willing to fly on Northwest, not United, for our next trip to the Philippines, in order to get a better deal on my ticket? *No way, Jose!* I respectfully declined with a flowery note, clarifying that the United miles were one of the job perks for my family, allowing us eventually to travel together, to make up for my frequent absences.

I called Bonnie, the publisher of *The Reel Directory*, and told her that my listing in her media professionals' guide had gotten me this amazing opportunity to direct a movie abroad. She often ran ads about cool jobs her listees had landed, but this was exceptional. I promised to call her to provide details after the shoot.

John N, a good friend and former roommate from my film school days at Stanford, had recently finished editing the soundtracks for *Dragon: The Bruce Lee Story*. He invited me to a pre-release screening, then impressed me with special punch and fight sound effects he had created. John N had edited many low-budget features and constructed the sound tracks for many high-budget ones at Fantasy Films in Berkeley. He sent Mr. K an attractive bid to edit *Emerald Knight*, and we made plans for post-production editing and sound work in Berkeley. Kurosawa loved the idea of spending several months in California while we finished the film, and my family loved the idea of having me home.

I opened an account at Sanwa Bank's Berkeley office, which would enable Kurosawa to wire my weekly payment directly from his account at Sanwa Japan. This would be especially useful when we were shooting together abroad.

2nd Trip to Manila

For my second eight-day scouting trip to the Philippines in mid-February, I arrived in Manila after midnight. John McD and Toshi had flown in from Japan earlier that day. Kurosawa took me to a guesthouse, more modest than our last digs at the Manila Midtown Hotel. My room had a tropical feel, heavily rattaned and wickered, quite spacious, with a kitchen. I opened one of the cabinets, though, and the light spilling in disturbed the sleep of a dozen multi-legged critters, who scurried away indignantly. *Ugh.*

"I can't stay here," I told Kurosawa, who was standing across the room.

"What?"

"I can't stay here, Kurosawa-san, I'm sorry." I opened another cabinet as he came over, saw the bugs, and called the Ramada to get me a room.

174

Kurosawa, for some reason, stayed by himself at the Sheraton, a mile away.

Jun, the assistant director, was installed in a two-bedroom flat in Robinson's Garden Apartments, on the other side of Robinson's Place Mall from my hotel. He lived there with two 2nd assistant directors—Takai and Dai-ichi—and a production manager-cook named Yokoyama. A placard in one bedroom had the same curious "skillful and attractive masseuses" promo as my hotel room. A couple of days later, John and Toshi tired of the bugs at the rattan place and moved in downstairs from the assistants.

At first I thought some of the Filipino staff were calling me "Dreck," the Yiddish word for excrement, but I didn't think I was doing such a shitty job. I soon realized it was "Direc," short for Director. In the informal style of American crews, I had asked to be addressed by my first name. But the Japanese assistants balked at calling me "Bill."

"They're not sure what to call you," John confided to me one evening at the office. "They have only worked with autocratic Japanese directors before, and they are mostly used to addressing each other by their family names." In fact, when I had asked John for Kurosawa's first name during our initial talks, he didn't remember and most of the employees didn't know.

"The assistants want to call you Zarchy-san," he said.

Too formal, but these guys might be having trouble with the L's in my name. Eventually they bravely settled on "Mr. Bill."

Jun's apartment also served as the production office, rather modest digs for a feature film. We planned to rent office space in Ermita, close to many of the locations, as soon as funding came through from Tokyo. It was Kurosawa's job to get the rest of the money we needed for filming from Mr. H, the distributor-investor.

I felt a bit isolated by myself at the Ramada, but our international stars would eventually be joining me there during our shoot. My hotel was only a twelve-minute walk, through Robinson's Mall, to the office in Jun's apartment. Robinson's had several movie theatres, a pharmacy, food store, and clothing stores. During the day, when the place was filled with shoppers and families, it was a high-energy scene, fun to walk through.

One night, on my way up to the production office, the elevator suddenly lurched to a stop between floors. I assumed the failure was caused by a power brownout, and I wondered if this small building would have a back-up generator, but we started up again in a couple of minutes. When we arrived on the fourth floor, I was assured, "It's not a power problem, Boss, just a stuck elevator. Too much weight."

The power did go out during our production meeting later that evening, and we finished up by candlelight.

Hiring Crew

We began to hire more local crew people. Though dozens of films were made each year in Tagalog for the local market, Filipino crews loved the higher pay on international films like ours. For foreigners, production was still cheaper here than many places in Asia. Because the Philippines had been an American colony for fifty years, English was still the dominant language of commerce.

Kurosawa and I signed our letter of agreement that night. We had agreed that I would receive two percent of the "worldwide net profit" of *Emerald Knight* from all sources of revenue, with payments starting no later than three months after its release. I reserved the right to approve the final cut of the movie, and he agreed to fly me to the World Premiere, wherever that might be. At last I knew this was really going to happen, and I felt confident about my role. *I know how to do this,* I often thought during that second visit.

Archie told me that he was waiting for money from Kurosawa, to start building sets and to rent a production office and the camera, lighting, and sound gear we needed for our shoot, but so far he had no funds to work with, other than a small initial payment. I asked Kurosawa about this later, and he assured me money was coming from Japan very soon. He sounded very optimistic, and nothing could dampen my mood at that point.

Our local crew drifted slowly away, and I bid my hardworking Japanese assistant directors good night, walked down the four flights (no more elevators tonight!), and headed for my hotel. I was all aglow as I walked through the darkened mall.

Here I am, Mr. International Movie Guy, leading this merry band of film people from three continents. Most of this crew has more experience working on movies than I do.

I felt I could do the job, and I reveled in the challenge. They all looked up to me, literally. They trusted me and had confidence in me.

I'm Mr. World Traveler, comfortable in all sorts of situations, mellow master of my domain, able to flit from culture to culture with nary a blink.

A lone blue car approached me across the parking lot as I strutted toward the Ramada in the distance. Two guys cruised slowly by and sized me up carefully. Everything stopped at once—the blue car, my breathing, my heartbeat. Suddenly I felt much less full of myself, much more vulnerable.

Shit. I'm outside the safety zone, away from the hotels and eating places, beyond the reach of the tourist cocoon. A wave of kidnappings is afflicting this country. Do I look like the struggling filmmaker I am, or a rich, ransomable foreigner?

The car turned and sped off in another direction, and I looked around me with a shudder, unnerved by the cloying darkness of the mall at night. The power was off all around us, but a little sliver of light from the waning moon poked bravely through the thick air, and I felt very exposed. The Filipinos I dealt with daily were warm and sweet and immensely supportive of our effort to plan and shoot our movie, but I knew the mind-bending poverty surrounding us bred crime, and the ubiquitous armed guards were there for a reason. Not that I had a lot of confidence in pistol-packing teenagers.

I startled myself by stumbling over a curb, then hurried on to my hotel.

After that night, Archie made sure I always had a ride to the hotel, or Gene or one of the other production assistants would walk me home. Too creepy to walk alone at night, especially when the power was off.

Around this time, one of our Filipino staff took me aside and confided in me. "I don't usually like working with Japanese," he said. "They can be pushy and demanding. But these people are nice, not arrogant, and that creates a basis for trust."

Let's hope so, I thought.

Scouting Subic Bay

We set out to scout the former U.S. Naval Base at Subic Bay, several hours from Manila. We had planned a 6 a.m. departure, so we could drive there, look for locations, and travel home in one day. But it took a long time to round everyone up, as Toshi and the ADs had gone out carousing the night before. Eventually we hit the road, literally. Lousy paving repairs—*BAM!*—caused rhythmic bumps every 50 yards or so—*BAM!*—some gentler, some bone-rattling—*BAM!* Eventually we made it to Olongapo, a port-of-call for American naval vessels for nearly a century on the west coast of the island of Luzon.

During the previous year, Subic Bay and other U.S. installations had been evacuated to avoid the ash and other effects of Pinatubo, the nearby volcano whose enormous eruptions in 1991-92 had affected weather patterns worldwide. After American personnel and their families left, the Philippine Senate refused to renew the leases for several bases. With the U.S. Navy packed up and gone, Olongapo was a ghost town.

We cruised Ramón Magsaysay Drive, the main drag through the city, named for a popular president of the Philippines who was killed in a plane crash in the 50s (I remembered collecting a U.S. stamp honoring Magsaysay during my philatelic youth). Magsaysay Drive was lined with bars, strip clubs, eating places, inexpensive hotels—the kinds of businesses that appealed to young sailors on leave. Most were closed, some boarded up.

John explained that the Philippine government hoped to rebuild Subic Bay as a free-trade port, bringing in manufacturing, commercial import-export businesses, and resort properties. The government was also happy to assist us in using the base as a location. *Emerald Knight* would be the first international feature film to shoot at Subic, and Kurosawa had talked of setting up a feel-good meeting and press conference for us with Philippine President Fidel Ramos.

Once they found the keys and we gained access to the base, we found hundreds of buildings of all sizes and shapes—hangars, barracks, sheds, garages, shelters. Military development in that location dated back to the Spanish in the 1800s. Much of the infrastructure was old and had been neglected for years.

But Subic Bay had vast stretches of concrete with little or no plant life. The central part of the base contained nearly 60,000 acres, miles and miles of roads, bridges, paved lots, runways for military aircraft, wharves and landing areas for ships. Except for landscaped areas around barracks and other living quarters, there were oceans of concrete in every direction.

Of course, upon close inspection, there were many areas, typical of the tropics, where plant life was struggling to break through, exploiting or creating cracks in the solid concrete. *That's fine,* I thought. *Brian has already written a scene in the script that uses foliage in cracks in a paved road as a visual metaphor for freedom from oppression.*

Subic provided a great bleak look for us. There was lots of room to move around, a hangar in which to build a set for Dirk's apartment (he had to have a home, after all), and other buildings with steel stairways and boiler rooms in which to film fights. There was space for us to stage pyrotechnics, crane shots, helicopter shots, and vehicle chases, without seeing the foliage that surrounded this massive island of concrete. I thought about my friend's warning and wondered if I could stay out of choppers.

We planned to blow up half a dozen vehicles and a number of small, improvised buildings. Popoy, the pyro guy, asked about my preferences: "How do you want us to blow things up, Direc? With explosions or implosions? Do you want flames or smoke? Or both? Black smoke or white?" All of this was quite modest by the standards of a Schwarzenegger action flick, of course.

But we have Dick Fly! And me. So many decisions.

We had to shoot at Subic, that was clear to everyone, but bringing all the people and stuff we needed from Manila was an added travel expense and schedule extension Kurosawa hadn't counted on. He vowed to get the money and make it all work, and his optimism was contagious.

"It's pretty clear, isn't it, that our shoot will need five weeks, not four?" I asked. He concurred.

Corregidor

We took a boat to tadpole-shaped Corregidor Island, in the mouth of Manila Bay, a strategic base during World War II, when the Philippine archipelago was still an American colony. In fact, Corregidor was the place where General MacArthur uttered his famous "I shall return," one of the great exit lines, as he left for Australia when the Japanese bombarded, invaded, and conquered Corregidor in 1942. Three years later, the Americans bombarded, invaded, and reconquered the island.

We drove past bombed-out ruins of American barracks, a Japanese Peace Garden, the newly opened Filipino Heroes Memorial, the huge steel Flame of Freedom sculpture, and the U.S.-built Pacific War Memorial, all against a sparkling setting of verdant hills and sweeping views of Manila

Bay. I looked around at my crew, my new Japanese and Filipino friends. "Now we're all making a movie together," I said, as we smiled at each other.

The beauty of the setting, the creepy old memories of Japanese, Filipino, and American blood shed there, and the modern expressions of peaceful good will combined to move us all. . The war seemed quite remote at that point.

At the same time, I was aware of being the only American in the group. Most of the time that didn't matter, but sometimes the language and cultural gaps seemed overwhelming. Besides the size thing, I wondered how often Akebono felt awkward culturally, a mixed-race American expat in a nearly all-Japanese sport.

We entered the Malinta Tunnel, a massive, bombproof bore through the center of the island, originally built as an arsenal and military hospital, and later the headquarters of the American high command. The main tunnel was over eight hundred feet long, 24 feet wide, with 24 long branch tunnels, each 15 feet wide.

I immediately saw the potential for using parts of Malinta for some of the tunnels in our film. Archie and Romy assured me that securing this location would be no problem, even though it was a national monument. I became a bit obsessed with the idea. Here was another great, bleak location, with vast expanses of concrete and steel.

George Lucas used parts of the unfinished Bay Area Rapid Transit system's tunnels when he shot his early sci-fi film, THX-1138. We have to have the Malinta Tunnel!

Since we still had several weeks before we started shooting, I was slated to fly home again, and John was heading back to Tokyo. Kurosawa would stay on in Manila with the ADs. Before I left, we returned to the Comelec Building, where a film crew was shooting. A prominent Filipino director named Cirio Santiago (who made three movies a year) was filming a prison scene on the set we had watched them build on our last visit. My

Japanese friends were interested to watch the crew of Pinoys, as Filipinos call themselves.

I know that my guys from Tokyo are a bit smug. They think they'll have to teach the locals a thing or two.

This is the same attitude that people from L.A. or New York bring with them when they come to shoot in San Francisco and hire local crew people, like me.

"What a cow town," they complain to each other. "These guys don't even know how to defigulate a left-handed framistan ..." or "God, I can't even get free-range organic arugula here ..."

Thus sensitized, those of us from San Francisco then go shoot in smaller markets, like Kansas City, hire local crews, and gripe: "What a cow town..."

It's not about how big a fish you are. It's about the size of your pond. Actually, Kansas City really is a cow town.

Jun and Toshi and the others watched the Filipino crew complete a scene and check the camera. "Let's move to Scene 27B," barked the assistant director, and they all raced to the next angle. Three grips lifted a 30-foot dolly track, spun it around, and shifted it way over to the right. Two other guys rolled some big lights across the set, a young electrician leaped up a tall ladder and refocused a couple of hanging lights, the camera crew reloaded film and changed lenses and positions, the sound people moved mics and fishpoles, the actors started running through lines and blocking the next scene. Lickety-split, not a wasted minute. I looked at my guys from Tokyo.

Clearly they're impressed. I wonder if they'll be able to keep up.

Our final scout on that trip was to an infamous hellhole named Smokey Mountain, the main garbage dump for millions of Manilans. You could tell when you were in the vicinity of Smokey Mountain. Noxious smoke from nonstop garbage fires and the stench of rotting, burning, and toxic refuse wafted for miles in every direction. Manila's usual blanket of brown air thickened here into an unbreathable acrid pea soup, yet thousands of squatters lived in tin-and-cardboard shanties among smoldering refuse, some making as much as $10 a day picking trash. Generations of families lived here and children grew up here, no doubt poisoned by this poor excuse for air.

"You wanted severe-looking locations, Boss," Romy said, "Do you want to shoot here?"

"No way," I gasped. "Get me away from here as quickly as possible."

"But, Boss, there are no plants around here. Not many, anyway."

"No! Away! Now!"

Before I headed back to San Francisco, Archie took me aside.

"Bill, I still have no money to rent the production office and to set up rental of the camera equipments. I'm worried. Can you please talk to Mr. Kurosawa and stress to him that the situation is serious? I need cash to keep the wheels of the movie turning." I did speak to Kurosawa, and he assured me he would be getting another payment on his budget in a few days.

At the airport on the way out, I bought a set of colorfully painted, stylized, wooden jungle animals for my kids—elephant, zebra, leopard, tiger, and others—which in an odd way symbolized for me our Japanese-Filipino-American-Canadian-Dutch production. I also bought a Corregidor T-shirt depicting the Flame of Freedom for my wife, and for myself, a white T-shirt with a colorful jeepney filled with happy, smiling Pinoys. The license plate read: "2.25.86," the date Ferdinand Marcos was deposed as president of the Philippines.

Back Home Again

I was busy during my two-and-a-half weeks at home. I had asked

Kurosawa's company to rent me a Macintosh laptop to help me organize the shoot. John called: "How would you feel about buying a laptop yourself and renting it to the production?" I found a six-month-old Mac PowerBook (then very new) for sale from a guy in San Francisco and paid him $1,600 in cash.

It was a lot of dough to lay out. No one I knew had laptops then, but I thought it would help me organize the production, keep track of the script, and perhaps even do some of the graphics for the film. Kurosawa would pay me rental for a few weeks, and I promised Susan I would sell the computer right away if the project fell through.

I received my second $2200 payment from Kurosawa in a wire through Sanwa Bank.

At least some money is flowing from the production.

I arranged to get together with Monika and her boyfriend, Mars. They took the one-hour flight from Burbank to Oakland, and we chatted at the airport coffee shop. She had won the International Super Model of the Year Award seven years before, at age 14, and appeared in *Sports Illustrated's* swimsuit issue at 15. She was over six feet tall, unglamorous in jeans with no makeup. I knew from experience on Macy's commercials that fashion models like her could show up for a shoot in the morning with slept-in hair and sleepy faces, and appear quite plain, even funny looking. But these drab caterpillars, when painted and dolled up, emerged as fabulous silken butterflies, because they possessed the kind of arresting light eyes, perfect nose, and photogenic, high-cheekboned look the camera loved.

Monika was concerned, and full of questions. "Is this really going to happen? Doesn't this film seem like a flaky deal? The pay is way below what I make modeling, and for six weeks! What other movies have you directed?"

"Oh, this is my first time directing a feature. I'm really a DP. I got hired through a listing in a media directory. Kurosawa liked a music video I shot with MC Hammer." I thought it was a great story, but this did little to reassure her.

Monika had action scenes in the script, so I was relieved to hear that she had studied kickboxing for about a year. "Don't worry, it's definitely happening," I soothed. "I've been to Japan and the Philippines, met the people, seen the locations, stayed in the hotels. They're over there right now, making plans and spending money."

As I assured her, I wondered if Kurosawa had come up with the cash yet. I didn't feel dishonest, just ... optimistic. She told me Mars would accompany her on the shoot and asked if he could have a small part. No problem. Again I cast an actor I barely knew without an audition. It was a small price to pay to keep her happy. We agreed to stay in touch and I ended on an up note: "See you in three weeks in Manila!"

I prepared to be away nearly two months, ten days of pre-production planning plus nearly six weeks of principal photography. This would be my longest trip ever away from my family. I hugged and kissed Susan and my son Danny, and threw my gear in the back of the airport shuttle, but my older boy Razi hadn't come home from fourth grade before we had to drive off. At the end of the block, I spotted him crossing the street from school, and the van driver pulled over so I could jump out and hug him goodbye.

3rd Trip to Manila

I arrived in Manila well after midnight again for my third visit. Kurosawa met me and we stayed up late drinking beer in the Ramada's lobby bar, which remained open until the last customer left.

He was glum. "Our money people in Japan are not happy that shoot will take so long," he said. I was disturbed that John and Toshi were both still in Tokyo, but he assured me they would arrive in a few days.

Meanwhile, he told me, many of our Filipino crew people would be around the office this week as we planned all phases of our shoot. Casting for smaller parts had been going on for days and would continue at nine in the morning. The casting director was an American guy named Nick.

"You meet Nick tomorrow. You will like Nick," Mr. K assured me with a chuckle. "He's American, like you."

I fell into my room. It was after two a.m., and I wanted to set up and check my computer. But my head was swimming from too much beer, my back was aching from too much airplane, and I dialed the skillful and attractive masseuse line.

Helen was attractive enough, I guess, but her skillfulness was quickly put into doubt when she began an aggressive thumb assault on my body. I realized this was a clumsy attempt at shiatsu and stopped her. "No, no. No shiatsu. Swedish, please. Swedish."

She broke out the oils and started to soothe and stretch my tired back and leg muscles, relieving the strain of 18 hours in economy class seating plus four hours of airport limbo during a layover in Seoul. I turned over and she worked on my arms, shoulders, chest, thighs, and calves. Heavenly. She paused a moment.

"Do you want special service?" Naively I asked what that was.

She reached down, grabbed me and said, "By hand."

Whoa. Where have those hands been? No thanks.

I couldn't sleep, despite the massage and my exhaustion, so I unpacked my PowerBook and printer. My body was confused by the time change, my mind preoccupied and worried. Was my lack of experience hurting the project? For distraction, I got down on the floor and examined the two kinds of electrical outlets in my room. One looked American and the other European, but when I carefully measured their voltages, nothing was as expected. I decided to ask for help in the morning, but I was able to use the PowerBook on battery to kill time for hours playing "Spectre," my favorite tank battle game.

Still awake at five-thirty, I opened my curtain. The sun would be up in less than an hour, and the sky was starting to lighten. The mountains of the Bataan peninsula in the distance were just starting to catch the crimson skylight, proving once again that pollution makes for fabulous sunrises. I finally crawled into bed, slept fast, and popped awake three hours later. The power was out, so I had one light, a cold shower, and a ten-minute wait for the emergency elevator, while the floor watcher struggled to stay awake in the hallway.

Casting

At nine a.m. I arrived at the office, already crowded with job seekers, actors, and wannabes there to impress us. The outer room hushed when I entered. Few knew I was the director, but I stood out in that crowd like Akebono in Tokyo. I smiled at them. *Good morning.* They smiled back. Clearly they didn't know, or care, how inexperienced I was. And I knew I could do this!

Nick, the casting director, *was* American, but that was the only way he was like me. An expat and former GI, he had come to Manila on R & R during Vietnam, met and married a Filipina, and stayed to raise a family. He had acted in and worked on lots of movies. He was tall, high-strung and volatile, with an energy level I wanted to keep on my side, but he knew lots of actors and was good at scheduling and making deals.

The local film industry had gotten its biggest boost when Francis Ford Coppola decided to shoot *Apocalypse Now* there in the mid-70s. Filming this Vietnam War epic took four years to complete. A typhoon destroyed a whole village of sets one year, and star Martin Sheen suffered a heart attack the next. After putting up with Hollywood people in the Philippines for a while ("What a cow town. I couldn't even get onion-fennel bagels and non-fat schmear in Manila ..."), Coppola's company hired dozens of capable Filipino craftspeople and trained them in the Hollywood style— unit managers, script supervisors, stunt coordinators, pyrotechnicians, lighting and grip crews, camera assistants, and audio recordists.

In the years since *Apocalypse*, many international movies had been shot in the Philippines, often faking the locations as elsewhere in Asia or Latin America. These included action pictures like *Missing in Action* and *Delta Force II* with Chuck Norris and eminent films like Peter Weir's *The Year of Living Dangerously*, Oliver Stone's *Platoon* and *Born On the Fourth of July*, and Taylor Hackford's *An Officer and a Gentleman*. On the other hand, during the same period, other crews in the Philippines shot *Ferocious Female Freedom Fighters*, *Perils of Gwendoline in the Land of Yik Yak*, and *Vampire Hookers*.

My Filipino crew had worked on many of the best jobs, and they paraded through our office over the next day or two as we plodded through the casting. We did have a number of small parts still to fill, but Nick's audition list was enormous. We saw several good character actors the first day and made most of our selections (including the cockroach eater), so I was dismayed to see how many people were scheduled for the second day.

"There are twice as many people on the list for tomorrow. Surely we can weed out some of these folks ahead of time," I said to my group.

Resistance from the ADs. "No, no, not a good idea, Mr. Bill. We need to see everybody."

Jun, Takai, and Dai-ichi fended off my attempts to shorten the list, and as the next day began, I could see why. The vast majority of the "actors" coming on the second day were babes. Gorgeous, dark-eyed Filipinas with long, lustrous dark hair, 15 to 20, many with no acting experience, short, lithe, nubile, demure yet sexy in this most Catholic of countries. My boys were entranced. I drifted away during the second afternoon of casting.

These girls are lovely and dying to get noticed. They don't need me.

I was disappointed to hear from Archie that we couldn't shoot at Corregidor after all, since it was "a national monument, of course" and unavailable. He seemed to have forgotten his earlier assurances that we would get permission to film on the island. But where could we get our tunnel shots? We'd have to find places to fake them at Subic.

The start of filming approached. We hired a stunt coordinator, a lanky, powerful guy named Gil with a big smile and crooked teeth, and we discussed plans for various fights and ways to stage action around Dick's strengths and Monika's untested kickboxing skills.

We hired a mature Filipino assistant director named Hernan, in addition to our three young Japanese ADs. An avuncular type with a gentle manner, Hernan would translate and coordinate our decisions and logistical moves to the local crew, including his daughter Nelia, our script supervisor. Our pyro guy, Popoy, hung around the office and offered many suggestions for all phases of the production. When we were discussing whether he and his crew should be with us in Subic for the entire shoot or just for the days when we were blowing things up, he looked at me, grinned, and said, "We all help each other, Direc. We'll be there the whole time." Manny, our transportation coordinator, brought pictures of military vehicles we could rent, and Jeffrey, the art director, brought plans for the office and apartment sets.

Power Bars

The Japanese ADs went through the entire script with me word by word, line by line, trying to understand the subtlety of the writing and nail down production details. In a constant cloud of cigarette smoke, Takai, who spoke the best English, led the pack interrogating me.

"Mis-ter-Bill," he drew out in a slow, resonant baritone, "Dirk says in Scene 57, 'You, tie up Toda with that rope there.' But who does he talk to? Where is the rope? How long? What color? And why is there a rope in Toda's office?" I hadn't thought through these details so exhaustively, but surely I needed to. We put in many hours together trying to get it all straight.

I cut up a couple of Power Bars with my Swiss Army knife and put them out on a plate for the group to share. My Japanese friends were intrigued by the gesture, but a bit dismayed by the density and chewiness of the Power Bars.

"They're good survival food," I hold them. Takai snacked as he continued the cross-examination.

Now language was becoming a problem. I understood about two-thirds of what my Japanese friends said, and I knew they missed a lot from me. Many of my attempts at humor failed to amuse anyone, though when I explained a joke, they would smile or laugh politely. I told Kurosawa that I needed John there to help translate my work with the ADs. Besides that, where was Toshi? How could we start shooting soon without my DP?

Mr. K looked abashed, shuffled a bit, and assured me they would come soon. Now I was beginning to wonder.

The next day was Sunday. We all had the day off and planned to loaf around. I slept late and went for a walk along Manila Bay to massive Rizal Park. Thousands of families were out on a beautiful, sunny afternoon, and I wandered past fountains and fields and kids playing soccer, from the Manila Hotel on one end to the National Library on the other. A band played in a grove lined with flowers. I stopped to buy ice cream near a 50-foot memorial to Filipino patriot José Rizal. I looked around, my nervous system a-tingle, feeling very conspicuous, very much the Big American.

I've never been claustrophobic, but right now I feel pretty hemmed in.

I noticed a dozen guys doing some kind of patterned movement among the trees and strolled closer. At first I couldn't tell what they were doing, but then I realized the leader was Gil, our stunt guy. He saw me taking pictures, came over with a big smile, and shook my hand limply. "I teach this class here every week, to train young people to do stunts. It's free. Thank you for coming to see us!" Then he introduced me to his group. "This is Mr. Bill, the Direc of our movie."

The class staged a series of mock fights, attacks, martial arts drills, and drop-and-rolls, then Gil himself wowed his protégés by leading them in tumbling and sparring. I was impressed. This guy had been stunt coordinator for Oliver Stone and Chuck Norris on half a dozen flicks. Now he was working for me.

I thanked him warmly, told him I looked forward to the shoot, said goodbye to the class, and moved on.

My heart started to go pitter-pat. *So much stimulus for my poor tired brain!* I sweated buckets in the humid air. Shooting started in less than a week.

Summons to the Office

The next morning, my phone rang early. "My name is Jun," a familiar voice announced formally.

"G'Morning, Jun. Wassup?"

"Can Mr. Bill come please my office, meet Kurosawa-san? Very important." I was there in a flash, but Kurosawa wasn't. I waited around for hours, my dread increasing.

It could be something trivial, I thought, *but it probably isn't.* I feared bad news about the money. I called him at the Sheraton, but he was not in his room. Eventually he called me at the office that afternoon and asked me to meet him back at my hotel, in the lobby bar. I raced to the Ramada, found him, and we settled down to talk.

He'd been glum when I arrived in Manila, but I'd never seen him like this, downcast and defeated. "I am not able to get next payment from company that promised to invest in our production," he said. "Mr. H, the man you met at distributor office in Tokyo, was away in Cuba, where they have very bad phones, for two weeks, so I could not call him. But now he is back in Japan, and he does not call me back.

"I am afraid they have no longer confidence in us."

I had seen the signs earlier, but I had ignored them, trying to concentrate on my job and make a credible film with inexperienced stars picked by someone else. This was bad.

Kurosawa looked depressed and ashamed. "I have no more money to pay anyone, even you. I kept hoping and wanted to keep production going. I want to move out of Sheraton right away, but I cannot, because I have no money to pay bill.

"But I still hope. I ask you please fly home and wait a few weeks."

"Really?"

"I think I can work it out with Mr. H, and we can all come back in one month and make our shoot."

"What will you do?" I asked.

"Who knows?" he answered with a sad smile. "Maybe I marry a Filipina. They are very beautiful, and over 15,000 of them marry Japanese guys every year." *Another way this country exports people*, I thought.

"I think we must tell local crew today," he said, "and ask them wait one month for us, not to take other jobs." My mind was spinning. Was I really going home? This was so sudden.

"I have asked Jun to call a meeting," he said. "They all come to the office at five o'clock."

About two dozen assembled in the apartment—Jun, Takai, Dai-Ichi, Yokoyama the cook, Archie, Romy, Nick, Gene the PA, Popoy the pyro guy, Gil, Hernan the AD, his daughter Nelia the script supervisor, Jeffrey the art director, Manny the vehicle guy, and others. They all knew something was up, but they were in good spirits nonetheless. Kurosawa thanked everyone for coming, then said, "I have asked Mr. Bill explain what is happening. My English is so poor."

I was astounded. *He never asked me to drop the news!* I knew he owed everyone money, and I would assume no responsibility for that. I was just as much a victim as my crew was. He had set me up. My heart pounded as I tried to figure out what to say. None of this was my doing, but I didn't want to embarrass anyone or cause bad feeling, in case we could continue the project in a few weeks.

I looked at the folks in front of me. I hemmed a bit, hawed a bit more, then repeated what he'd told me earlier, punctuated often with "or so Mr. Kurosawa says" and "as Mr. Kurosawa has *just* told me." I told them I was going home temporarily, and we hoped that they would be able to wait until we started up again soon. We had enjoyed working and planning with them, and we had come so close. In any case, it had been a memorable multicultural experience.

I thought I did pretty well for an off-the-cuff plea, avoiding responsibility while telling them what they needed to hear. The room was very quiet as they absorbed what I said. "And the money we are owed so far?" blurted Nick.

I wasn't touching that one. I gestured toward the boss.

"I pay you as soon as I have budget," said Mr. K. In other words, I have no money.

"Shit," yelled Nick. "I can't believe it! I've been fucked before, and I'm getting fucked again. I wasn't gonna let this happen. Again!" He stormed out of the room.

The meeting broke up. Hernan came up to me with a smile. "Nelia and I will wait. We will turn down work on other international films. It is hard to do more than one picture before the rainy season starts, and we would love to work with you." Gene said he would wait too, and asked if I thought it would really happen in a month.

"All I know is what he tells me," I answered. Other people offered gestures of support. Some left in silence. Soon they had all drifted away, and I was alone in the apartment with the Japanese guys.

Malaise

With nothing else to do, I hung out in the office with them. The mood was subdued. Kurosawa huddled with Jun and Takai. He wanted them to stay for the next month and keep working. Dai-ichi went out on an errand, and Yokoyama, the production manager-cook, began cutting up onions.

My brain struggled to grasp what had happened, to guess what was going to happen. My dreams of flying off to glitzy movie premieres all across Asia were crumbling. I was suddenly out of work. A feeling of malaise grabbed me in the *kishkas*. I picked up a week-old English-language newspaper and read every word in it for the tenth time, including the ads.

There was beer, but I didn't want to get drunk. I wanted to get high, but there was no weed. After a while, I bummed a cigarette and lit up. It was a Camel, my first tobacco in many years, and it felt strangely mellow to inhale. I pretended it was a joint and held the smoke in, but this produced an unpleasant dizziness. Nothing like getting high, but strangely close enough under the circumstances. I started to cough. Kurosawa had been watching me in amazement. He came over and made a small bow.

"I am very sorry," he said solemnly. "I have made you to be a smoker."

Yokoyama produced a pork curry, and we were surprisingly hungry. We chatted quietly over dinner, and I felt the language barrier more than ever. Despite all my time with the Japanese guys, we could still only communicate in a limited way, complex ideas were difficult, and humor was impossible. John, who was supposed to be my linguistic and cultural bridge, was still in Tokyo, and I realized he wouldn't be coming at all, not this time.

Suddenly there was a banging on the door. It flew open, and there stood Nick, filling the doorway with beer in hand, eyes intense. It was clear that he had had a few. "We had our own meeting, and we decided to come back." He looked huge.

Little Gene slid in around him. "We all talked it over. We thought you must be feeling bad, so we decided to come back and have a party to cheer you up." He produced a case of San Miguel, and more people started to arrive.

Incredible. They've worked for us for weeks, some without pay, possibly never getting paid, and they're worried that we're feeling bad?

Gotta love these people!

Many of our Filipino crew arrived with more beer, someone put on music, and we partied for the next couple of hours. I just knew we would return soon to shoot *Emerald Knight*.

A Quiet, Neighborhood Bar

About eleven o'clock, I was tired and starting to think about my bed at the Ramada. Our guys were getting organized about something, and Archie approached me.

"Direc, we're leaving in a minute to go to a club, and we wanted to know if you would come with us."

"I don't know, Arch, I'm pretty tired. It's been an exhausting and emotional day."

"Well, I can bring you back to the Ramada whenever you're ready to leave. We'd be honored if you would come out with us for a while. The name of the club means 'My Place' in Tagalog. It's a quiet, neighborhood bar quite close to here. Dai-ichi's girlfriend works there."

I should have known better. It was a strip club, a go-go bar, where listless babes danced topless to loud rock-and-roll, looking bored, then mingled with the customers. I watched for a few minutes, unimpressed.

I wish I were home with my wife and my little family, or at least back in my hotel room. The place was loud and smoky and my companions seemed committed to getting much drunker than I did. Clearly they had spent many hours together at My Place. Dai-ichi's "girlfriend" was a bar girl he'd dated a few times.

While I gabbed for a while with Romy and Nick, who were ogling the dancers, I noticed Archie and Mr. K talking with an older woman, gesturing toward me. I turned to my right and came nose-to-nose with a pretty, young Filipina wearing only a g-string. She had pulled up a chair next to me and was sitting very close.

"Hello," she said. I was aware that my friends were all watching.

"My name is Christina. What's your name?"

"Uh, I'm Bill."

"How old are you?" A common query from Filipinos.

"46. And you?"

"I'm 16."

What do I say to a topless bar girl in Manila who is 30 years my junior and has probably grown up and lived her whole life within a few miles of this table?

The desire to converse ended when she put her hand on my thigh and flashed a sweet smile. I stammered a little, excused myself, and went to the "comfort room," the toilet. When I returned, I sat by Archie.

"What's going on here, Arch?" I liked to call him "Arch," like Meathead to Archie Bunker in *All in the Family*.

"Going on? What do you mean?"

"I mean, what's the deal with the girl?"

"Deal? There is no deal. The place closes at four a.m. If you're still here and want her to go home with you, make a deal then. But if you decide to do that, I would be very careful about disease."

"I should say so!" A thought occurred to me. "My God, do they even sell condoms in this country?"

"Oh sure, Boss. The government makes sure they are sold everywhere, in pharmacies and food stores. Even the Church can't stop that."

Silence between us. The Eagles' "Hotel California" blared from the club's speakers as the girls on stage jiggled distractedly.

"Listen, Arch, I'm sure she's very nice."

"So?"

"So ... I mean ... I don't want to offend anyone. But I'm married, not interested. She's just a child. And no one should have to do what she does."

He turned and smiled at me. "Okay, Direc. I'm going to leave pretty soon and head home. I haven't seen my wife in a few days. Now it looks like I'll have some time off. Do you want a ride back to your hotel?"

"Thank you." I said goodbye to Christina, who looked disappointed, and to the group. Nick and Romy were boisterously enjoying the attentions of some of the dancers. In freewheeling Manila, I felt like quite a prude.

Wrapping It Up

Next morning, my last day in the Philippines, we had planned to gather at nine to revisit some of our locations in town. Takai and Dai-ichi and some of our local crew had never seen the Comelec building in Intramuros, the ruins at Pasig, the warehouses and offices. There were still decisions to be made. Filming was postponed for a month, but we planned to proceed as if we were just facing a short break, to help keep our morale up.

Romy was missing, and our scout was pushed back till late morning. When he finally arrived, it was obvious he had been out all night with someone he had met at My Place. I knew he was married, but people here winked at such things.

"Did you find a nice girl, Romy?" I asked as we were riding to location.

"Oh yes," he said.

"Filipinas are very beautiful, aren't they?"

"Oh yes, Boss. That is why it's so hard for us to have just one."

We walked through the Comelec building. The shoot we had watched the month before was now just a whisper of memory for the old building. The Pinoy crew had dismantled most of their prison set, but parts of the cells had been left to blend in with the ruins.

I wonder if I'll ever lead a crew on a shoot in here.

We lunched at our McDonald's in Ermita and checked out the office building where we had planned to build sets and the holevator location in the vacant lot. My heart really wasn't into it, and the rest of the group was hung over and subdued.

I returned to the Ramada and called John in Tokyo. "What happened?" he asked. I had been planning to ask him that.

"I don't know exactly," I said. "But if Mr. H isn't returning Kuro-san's phone calls, that's bad." We promised to stay in touch in the next few weeks.

I headed back to my room to pack, fighting a headache. Hours later I felt tired and tense, called again for a masseuse, and enjoyed having the muscles in my back and shoulders basted and kneaded. I knew I could be offered a rub and a tug again, and this time I was ready. As we neared the end of the massage, she asked if I wanted the "extra service." I pointed out where I had left her tip on the dresser, rolled over onto my stomach, and went to sleep.

Back to San Francisco

On my flight home, I sat next to a U.S. Air Force colonel assigned as a military attaché to our embassy in Seoul. He told me harrowing stories of truce violations by North and South Korea that threatened the forty-year-old yet still-fragile peace agreements.

"Remember, Seoul is only twenty-five miles from the border," he said. "Two million troops face each other at the demilitarized zone. If the North Koreans overrun the border, they're in Seoul in an hour."

He thought my *Emerald Knight* adventure was fascinating and wished me luck. I found his stories of confrontation and possible war—like living in a Tom Clancy novel—much more real than the already-dreamlike experience I was leaving behind.

I came home to an empty house. Everyone was at school. I'd left for eight weeks and returned in eight days. I leashed the dog and headed to the Burger Depot, a local hangout. David, the owner, jumped when he saw me and said, "Hey, you're in Manila."

"Not any more I'm not. But I'm going back in a month."

"You watch out, you go back," said David, who's from Hong Kong. "They kidnap people. My cousin, he scared to stay there. They like to take Chinese."

A few weeks later, Kurosawa called from Manila to announce that he was officially shutting down the production and sending Jun and the others back to Japan. I don't think they ever got paid, nor did the Filipino staff. As promised, I sold the PowerBook. Mr. K called me several times over the next few months to report on the progress of our film, or the lack of same. He returned to Japan for about two weeks to sell his Maserati and his Mercedes for some ready cash. He said he saw Mr. H, the Tokyo distributor, and they nearly came to blows.

Kurosawa told me that his office assistant in Tokyo had stolen five million yen ($40,000 at the time) from a company bank account, and that some of our Filipino staff had withdrawn $30,000 from the movie's Manila account for a deposit on equipment that was never made. He also told me that the big villain in our funding crisis was a talent agent who represented some of the stars and had promised to invest in *Emerald Knight*, then reneged. I don't know how much of all this is true. John McD told me later that there was more money unaccounted for.

At some point I had to face the possibility that perhaps the funding had fallen through because they lacked confidence in *me*, given my light track record as a director. Perhaps I had been the problem, a depressing thought for sure. Ironically, my confidence had increased steadily as we had gotten closer to shooting ... and the eventual shutdown.

Epilogue

I never went back to the Philippines or saw Kurosawa again. The last I heard, he was living in Manila, sharing a house with some of our Filipino crewmembers, but that was years ago. As far as I know, he never produced another film, and he never paid me the $2,200 he owed me for my final week's work on the film. I don't know if he ever married a Filipina.

In three trips to the Philippines, I did score over 43,000 miles on United in eight weeks and I did use them for family trips. I earned every mile the hard way, with my butt squeezed into economy class seats. How *did* Akebono do it? Not in coach, for sure. Jet-setting around to exotic film premieres never became an option, but *Emerald Knight* did represent a career turn for me, the beginning of 20 years of shooting projects all over the world.

Six months after I left Manila, a film for a Japanese electronics company brought me back to Tokyo. We hired John McD as our production assistant. He was grateful for the work, and it was good to see him again. On Halloween night, John and I went out to dinner with Brian the scriptwriter. Rehashing the demise of *Emerald Knight* helped me get closure for the project.

We went to a party at a Brazilian nightclub, and my mind had trouble digesting the cultural casserole. Japanese, American, and Brazilian girls danced with men of all nationalities in costumes and masks, with samba music and eight-dollar Heinekens, at a Halloween party in Tokyo. What continent was I on? Somehow, I found my way home on the JR train. For the party, Brian lent me an evil-smelling monkey mask, which he didn't want back at the end of the evening. It deteriorated on the wall of my home in California for years until it became too foul to have around.

John McD and Brian and I still stay in touch. I've seen John a couple of times on return visits to Japan. He and his wife have two kids now and he works for a utility company as a translator and editor. Brian moved to Sydney with Yumiko, and works in online media there.

Monika Schnarre appeared in a dozen films and a dozen TV series during the 90s. She still acts and works as a TV host in Toronto and has recently come out with a new line of clothing for tall women, eyewear, and skincare products.

Subic Bay has been developed as a tax- and duty-free commercial zone, one of the main engines of the Philippine economy.

Emerald Knights is the name of an animated superhero film released in 2011, based on the Green Lantern comic book character.

I found out much later that Dick Fly's last name was really Vrij, pronounced *fry*, which means "free" in Dutch. I don't know why Kurosawa's team called him Dick Fly, which had all sorts of nasty overtones in English. He fought another seven years on the Rings circuit but never got to star in a movie. And I never got to direct one. *Emerald Knight* was not the Big Break I'd been waiting for.

It took a while for that to sink in. Once it was clear to me, I called Bonnie at *The Reel Directory* and told her there would be no story about the amazing job I had gotten through her media guide.

It *was* a flaky deal, after all.

India
Hong Kong
Malaysia
Uganda

Outroduction: Getting Randy

Once I began to get Randy, my writing juices started to flow again.

The only "real job" to interrupt my long freelance career was a six-year stint as staff director of photography at One Pass Film & Video in San Francisco, starting in 1982. In my second month there, One Pass acquired another company, The Kenwood Group, which came bundled with their staff director Randy Field.

Randy and I bonded immediately. With similar East Coast, spoiled-Bar-Mitzvah-boy backgrounds, I was able to "get" his clever, sardonic, often scatological, sometimes adolescent, frequently phallic, Mel Brooksian sense of humor, and there was something about his dead-pan Walter Matthau looks and delivery that tickled my funny bone. In addition, we both hated lazy creativity and refused to make the same film over and over again for different clients.

Our first shoot together came early one morning on a San Francisco sidewalk. I'd been up all night at the hospital with my wife on a false-labor scare, weeks before our first child was born. Of course I was tired as I shouldered the camera for a long, backwards walking shot leading an actor down the sidewalk, but I settled into the work, enjoying the comic nature of the script (an oddball skit urging college students to repay their student loans) and the light approach Randy brought to the set.

During that shoot, he took me aside at one point and said, "Listen, I went to film school, but it was a while ago, and I'm afraid I don't know what the hell I'm doing. So watch my back. If it looks like I'm gonna do something stupid, let me know. Subtly. Maybe a hand signal of some kind. Or a head shake."

Point taken, though I wasn't sure if he was kidding me. I'm still not. To this day, he visits my Advanced Cinematography classes at San Francisco State each year and reveals his two secrets of successful directing:

1. Always hire people who are smarter than you are

2. You must have a plan. It doesn't even have to be a good plan, as long as you start with a plan.

On our second shoot together, Randy told everyone how I'd come right to the set from the hospital on the previous gig, embellishing and dramatizing and humorizing the tale, as I chimed in and added details. I noticed that crews and clients alike tuned into his brand of humor and enjoyed his jokes. He was open to suggestions from others, often responding, "That's not a particularly stupid idea," a line he somehow pulled off with grace and enthusiasm.

Randy and I developed a way of integrating a funny patter into our work on the set, which some compared to the bickering of an old Jewish couple. Part of the fun of working together was the telling and retelling of our shooting experiences.

We built our own legend. Each year—more work, more stories, more fun. Randy would say, "That reminds me very little of a time ..." and we were off on another verbal adventure. A happy crew was a productive crew, and the humor never got in the way of the work. In fact, it was an important component. One time, after a particularly difficult technical setup, I stepped off the set to fetch Randy, to have him watch a rehearsal with our new lighting scheme.

I found him near the food table in the green room, schmoozing with the talent, nervous corporate executives who had to appear handsome, relaxed, charming, articulate, confident, and believable on camera a few minutes later.

"I've been working hard out front," I whined to Randy, "while you're back here telling jokes."

"I'm not telling jokes," he snapped in earnest. "I'm building rapport. Getting them to relax. Really."

Jokes were told, rapport was built, decisions were made, projects were completed. Clients went home happy. Best of all, every day was different.

In the early 90s, after we had both rejoined the freelance world, Randy and I started traveling the globe together for a variety of corporate and high-tech clients.

I had worked on several projects overseas early in my career. In my first year as a freelancer in the mid-70s, I shot a travel film for Pacific Delight Tours, following a hundred tourist "geese" as they flew through their Orient Escapade, an eight-city vacation tour of the Pacific Rim. The following year, I worked on Fleetwood Mac's "Rumours" concert tour of Japan and Hawaii. But for 15 years after that, and all through my time at One Pass in the mid-80s, I hadn't worked abroad.

The first trip with Randy in 1993 was a mammoth, seven-week shoot for a Japanese electronics company through New Zealand, Japan, Taiwan, Singapore, Uganda, Switzerland, Spain, Brazil, and four locations in the U.S. We amused crewmembers on six continents, especially those in former British colonies, where *Randy* was slang for *horny.*

Later that year I was hired by a Japanese producer to direct a sci-fi, action-adventure movie in the Philippines, a project which took me across the Big Pond three times in eight weeks to Tokyo and Manila.

In subsequent years, Randy and I shot projects for Silicon Valley tech giants and European healthcare conglomerates, returning to Japan many times, plus multiple trips to Singapore, Switzerland, Brazil, India, Thailand, China, Hong Kong, France, England, Germany, Switzerland, the Netherlands, Belgium, and Costa Rica (Other clients have taken me on shoots in Ireland, Mexico, Bali, Norway, Italy, Macau, Indonesia, Canada, Mexico, and all across the U.S.). For a number of years, I did more shooting work out of town than at home.

Through all this, my oral history with Randy continued. But the tales were so rich that I wanted to write them down.

I had been a writer in my youth, and had grown up in the home of a prolific, published author: my dad had written over 30 books on crafts, hobbies, and the outdoors. But by the end of the century, I hadn't written anything for decades.

When I was a kid, I had extorted several family members to purchase 25-cent subscriptions to a Zarchy newspaper—*All the Latest Family News!*—which I produced on an ancient, wooden-cased, Monarch Pioneer portable typewriter my dad had given me, using multiple sheets of carbon paper. This endeavor lasted one or two issues as I pocketed the profits. In college, I was a reporter and managing editor for *The Dartmouth*, the campus daily, and founding editor of the first-ever *Dartmouth Course Guide*. Since finishing graduate film school at Stanford, though, my focus had been strictly visual, pun intended.

By Y2K, I wanted to start writing again, but my two-fingered typing, self-taught in my youth on the Monarch, had deteriorated badly. I had trouble hunting and pecking a simple email without frustration. I taught myself to touch-type with "Mavis Beacon Teaches Typing" on my Mac, and my improved hand skills helped me record my thoughts efficiently.

I wrote a daily journal during a three-week shoot in Costa Rica, Alaska, and India with Randy and others. Whenever I could, I uploaded these journal entries and some photos to my new website, alerting family and friends by email—a very early blog, though that term was not yet common in 2000.

Our friends and families appreciated the journals. Many of them didn't understand the nature of our jobs. After we returned from India, our producer Larry got married here in the Bay Area. In my journal I had included notes on how calmly Larry had dealt with difficult scheduling problems, aggressive skycaps, and recalcitrant bureaucrats. At the reception, his dad came up to me, pumped my hand, and thanked me for "finally explaining what the hell Larry does on all these shoots."

In 2002, I published my first piece in the modern era, "Polishing the Talking Head: The West Wing Documentary Special," in *American Cinematographer Online,* the Bible of our industry. Here I described camera and lighting techniques I'd used to interview three former presidents and a host of White House aides. That same year, I started teaching Advanced Cinematography and Lighting at San Francisco State University ... and my father died. At the very moment my career was expanding to include writing and teaching, my dad, a retired writer and teacher, slipped away at age 90.

Soon I published other tales from the road about adventures with Randy and others in India, Singapore, and Taiwan. Once the writing juices began to flow again, the flood never abated. In 2010 I started my Roving Camera blog (billzarchy.com/blog), where I serve up a varied writing smorgasbord on cinematography, lighting, digital cameras, production, travel, technology, iPhone apps, books, personal musings, and baseball.

In my writing, it's hard to know what to call the production process anymore. *Shooting* isn't always appropriate, especially when working with politicians. I can't go around telling people I've shot five presidents, even though it's true. Are we still *filming* even when it's not on film?

Videoing? Really? Some called it *taping* for a while, but we don't record on tape anymore, it's all on cards and drives. Are we *carding* or *driving?* It's a problem. I stick with *filming,* to the chagrin of some of my colleagues. And don't even get me started on *rolling.* Nothing actually rolls.

Along the way, besides the inimitable Mr. Field, I've had wonderful travel buddies on my international shoots, including: Jim Rolin, Lori Wright, Larry Lauter, Laura Marks, David Rathod, Anne Sandkuhler, Mush Emmons, Dan Smith, Rod Williams, Jane Hernandez, Louis Block, Phil Paternite, Texas Jon McDonald, Tokyo John McDonald, Brian Haverty, Tommy Oshima, Bob Zagone, Bill Couturié, Mark Pedersen, Dan Pinkham, Conrad Slater, Scott Compton, Peter Yaremko, Geralyn Pezanoski, Victoria Reichenberg, Chris Coughlin, Jim Lucas, Nancy Kelly, Darrell Flowers, Kenji Muro, Nancy Bardacke, Vance Piper, Mauricio Arias, Edd Dundas, Joan Storey, Bob Elfstrom, Kent Gibson, and Michael Collins.

We've been blessed with a fine bevy of "fixers"—producer colleagues in each country (some dear friends by now) who make all our local arrangements, hire our local crews, gear, and vehicles, and take care of our kibitzing, procuring, interpreting, explaining, and cajoling: Eric Chabassier in France, Andrew van Hoffelen in the UK and Europe, Sushil Bhatnagar in India, Andrew Leung in China, Richard Kipnis and Carole Hisasue in Japan, Ricca Galdeano and Mauricio Bartz in Brazil, Alex Muller-Elsner and Peter Nagu in Germany, Joanna Schatz in Mexico City, Xavier Gutiérrez in Costa Rica, Ian Vincent in Uganda and Kenya.

I am deeply grateful for the hard work, upbeat attitude, and passion for production shown by many hundreds of creative film and video artists on my crews (in this highly collaborative medium), both here in the San Francisco Bay Area and around the world—directors, producers, other DPs, camera operators and assistants, gaffers, electricians, key grips, sound recordists, video technicians, data wranglers, teleprompter operators, drivers, script supervisors, prop masters, set designers, makeup artists, dolly grips, crane operators—improvisational gypsies all, who expertly schlep their talents and their gear to each day's office, wherever it happens to be, put it all together in new and unique configurations, make magic, then strike their tents and move on.

"Exactly how long will it take to set up the next shot?" the producer asked my gaffer on a recent shoot.

"I don't know *exactly*," he responded with a grin. "I've never done exactly this shot before."

Indeed, every day is different, no day is boring. You've gotta have a plan.

Build rapport, watch my back, let me know if I'm doing something stupid.

Always hire people who are smarter than you are.

Acknowledgments

I've been very lucky. I was born with a good eye and a decent brain, into a family of educators that encouraged me, gave me every opportunity to succeed, and sent me to an Ivy League college. I've benefited from some timely breaks and fruitful associations that have opened up vast new areas in my career. I've had my share of frustrations with the ups and downs and uncertainties of the freelance life. And I've gotten to travel the world and work with clever, creative people on six continents.

Deepest thanks to:

My parents, Harry and Jeanette Zarchy, who raised me with intelligence, humor, self-assurance, optimism, and love. My dad was a Renaissance man who could do anything. While he taught art in a New York City high school for 30 years, he wrote, photographed, and illustrated three dozen books on crafts, hobbies, and the outdoors, many of which stayed in print for decades. My mom, who lived to almost 98, went back to college when I was in junior high, finished her degree, and embarked on a long career as a kindergarten teacher, an inspiration to us all.

My dear wife Susan, my life partner, who has always maintained her confidence in my various talents, even at times when they seemed in little demand, with thanks for the love, beauty, and music she brings into our lives every day. Our devotion deepens with each passing year.

My sons Razi and Danny, and son-in-law Bryan, who constantly amaze and inspire me with their innovative, surprising, and varied approaches to adulthood.

My sister Sue Fischer, who has always been a huge source of encouragement, my brother-in-law Jim Fischer, as well as Norm Godwin and many of my cousins, nephews and nieces, including especially Nathie Tieman, who carefully reads and comments on each story, blog post, and photo.

My first editor Naomi Lucks, who agreed to take me on and edit a few of my stories when I had just started to write again after a thirty-year hiatus. Naomi was the first publishing industry professional who saw potential in my writing. "If I didn't," she told me frankly at our first meeting, "this would be a very awkward conversation."

My friend and longtime writing mentor Larry Habegger and the other perceptive, analytical, funny writers in Townsend 11: Jennifer Baljko, Carol Beddo, Jacqueline Collins, John Dalton, Dana Hill, Barbara Robertson, Bonnie Smetts, Jacqueline Yau, and Y.J. Zhu. For years now I've shared my tales with this warm gaggle of authors, marveling at their diverse talents, relishing and rehashing their constructive feedback.

My friend, writer Jim Vaccaro, for first describing our epic bowling match as the "Showdown at Shinagawa."

Some of the tales in this collection were previously published on my Roving Camera Blog (billzarchy.com/blog) or in print, and in most cases have been substantially rewritten and updated.

"Wrecks and Pissers: The Bombay-Pune Road" was selected by Travelers' Tales as an Editor's Choice story in March 2003, then published in *Gobshite Quarterly* in August 2004. It won a Bronze Award in the Destination category in the Fourth Annual Solas Awards for Travel Writing in 2011.

The story "Showdown at Shinagawa: Bowling for Budget in Tokyo" was first published in *Kyoto Journal* #66, May 2007. It won a Bronze Award in the Travel and Sports category at the Sixth Annual Solas Awards for Travel Writing in 2012.

"21st Century Village: Telemedicine in Rural India" was first published in

Kyoto Journal #68, November 2007.

"Dog Years" was first published, in a different form and under a different title, in the anthology *Chicken Soup for the Soul: My Dog's Life*, April 2011.

Several of the stories were first published in *Film/Tape World*: "New Zealand: Living a Lie at Mrs. O'Brien's," October 2004; "Starstruck at Cannes: Shooting on the Red Carpet," August 2005; "Tokyo: Tale of the 33rd Floor," October 2003; "Singapore: No Worry, Chicken Curry," January 2004; and "Taiwan: Mr. Wong and the Universal Language," July 2003.

About the Author

BILL ZARCHY is a freelance director of photography, writer, and teacher based in San Francisco. He has shot film and video projects in 30 countries and 40 states, including interviews with three former presidents for the Emmy-winning *West Wing Documentary Special*.

Other credits include the Grammy-winning *Please Hammer Don't Hurt 'Em*, the feature films *Conceiving Ada* and *Read You Like A Book*, the PBS science series *Closer to Truth*, and countless high-end corporate projects for a wide variety of technology and medical companies.

His tales from the road, technical articles, and personal essays have appeared in *American Cinematographer, Emmy*, and other trade magazines, *Travelers' Tales* and *Chicken Soup for the Soul* anthologies, the *San Francisco Chronicle* and other newspapers and literary publications, as well as on his Roving Camera Blog (billzarchy.com/blog). For a number of years, he has belonged to the San Francisco-based writers' collective Townsend 11 (townsend11.com) and has contributed stories to each of their first three anthologies: *No Fixed Destination, No Set Boundaries,* and *No Definite Plans,* all available now as e-books at the Kindle, Nook, and iBooks stores.

He has an AB in Government from Dartmouth and an MA in Film from Stanford. He has taught Advanced Cinematography and Lighting to graduate students at San Francisco State University since 2002, as well as lighting workshops and classes at UC Berkeley, De Anza College, and the Art Institute of California-San Francisco.

Showdown at Shinagawa is his first book.

Visit *Showdown* online for videos and more photos:
showdownatshinagawa.com

Facebook Page: facebook.com/showdownatshinagawa

Email: billzarchy@gmail.com

Director of Photography site: billzarchy.com

Roving Camera Blog: billzarchy.com/blog

Photos

Visit *Showdown* online for videos and more photos—showdownatshinagawa.com

All photos Copyright © 2013 by Bill Zarchy unless otherwise credited. Most of the photos in which I appear were taken by coworkers or passersby. Credit given when I know who took them. Photos in collages are described clockwise (from upper left), and group photos are identified left to right.

Title Page—Ticket from Yuyuan Garden (Shanghai, China 2010); cookie fortune from Blessed Garden Restaurant (Berkeley, California)

Showdown at Shinagawa: Bowling for Budget in Tokyo—Shinjuku skyline; bowling trophy/photo by Larry Lauter; Shinagawa Lanes/photo by Jon McDonald (Tokyo, Japan 2000 and 2008)

Shanghai Lunch—Fish heads; Kung Pao Cartilage; food vendor (Shanghai, China 2010)

Wrecks and Pissers: The Bombay-Pune Road—Indian buses; cows; motorbike family; group photo of Sushil Bhatnagar, me, Larry Lauter, Randy Field (Maharashtra, Karnataka, and Tamil Nadu, India 2000, 2005)

China: Globalization with a Vengeance—Starbucks; street scene; newspaper vendor (Hong Kong and Shenzhen, China 2005)

New Zealand: Living a Lie at Mrs. O'Brien's—Air New Zealand boarding pass; NZ Work Visa; Randy Field and me in front of Mrs. O'Brien's (Wellington and Palmerston North, New Zealand 1993)

21st-Century Village: Telemedicine in Rural India—Dr. Sukumar; local man; village street (Tirupattur and Thirukolakudi, Tamil Nadu, India 2005)

Starstruck at Cannes: Morgan Freeman on the Red Carpet—me, with Morgan Freeman; view from top floor suite at Carlton Hotel; Mark Pedersen and me; Mallika Sherawat photo by bollywoodsargam.com (Cannes, France 2005)

Tokyo: The Tale of the 33rd Floor—Riverside tower; executive on phone; freeway at night (Tokyo, Japan 2011)

Singapore: No Worry, Chicken Curry—Me in a bunny suit with a Sony F900/ photo by Jon McDonald; original Raffles Hotel; crew in bunny suits: Me, Malik, Randy Field, Larry Lauter/photo by Jon McDonald (Singapore 2002)

Health: Our Most Important Product—Jogger passing pub (Manchester, U.K. 2011); neighborhood and trains (Tokyo, Japan 2011); carrying boy upstairs (Mexico City 2012); farm ducks (Colorado, U.S.A. 2009)

Taiwan: Mr. Wong and the Universal Language—Randy Field and me with my Arri 16SR at the Intelligent Highway control room/photo by Rod Williams (Taipei, Taiwan 1993)

Sweet Home Shenyang—David Rathod and me with Panasonic 3700; the band at the Paulaner Brauhaus; view from Kempinski Hotel room (Shenyang, China 2010)

Steve Jobs: Consuming the Apples—Keyboard; Apple storefront; group photo of Jim Rolin, U2's Bono, and me (Dublin, Ireland 2004)

Brazil: Some Days the Bear Eats You—Train station; skyscraper; lobby escalator; street scene; shooting at the station with Canon 5D Mark II/ photo by Mush Emmons (São Paulo, Brazil 2011)

Gigantic in Japan: A Tall Tale—Daibutsu statue/photo by Jon McDonald (Kamakura, Japan 2000); small hotel room/photos by Randy Field (Nagoya, Japan 2000)

Uganda: A World Together—Kids in yellow uniforms; group photo of Randy Field, James Tibenderana, and me/photo by Rod Williams (Kampala, Uganda 1993); group photo of me, James, and Randy/photo by Jim Rolin (London, U.K. 2004); village scene

Dog Years: Sophie, Pop, and Bill Clinton—President Clinton (New York 2002); Pop in his classroom (Brooklyn, circa 1955); Sophie (San Francisco, circa 1998); crew shot with Clinton

The Big Break: Malaise in Manila—Philippines map on bamboo tray; carved Filipino animals; Corregidor T-shirt (Manila, Philippines 1993)

Outroduction: Getting Randy—Randy Field and me shooting Sony Z1U on the street (Mandya, Karnataka, India 2005); me shooting Orient Escapade with a handheld Éclair NPR camera/photo by Edd Dundas (Hong Kong 1975); group arrival photo of Rod Williams, Jane Hernandez, and Randy Field (Entebbe Airport, Uganda 1993); me shooting the Éclair from a rickshaw/photo by Edd Dundas (Penang, Malaysia 1975)

About the Author—Photo by Toshihiro Oshima (Tokyo, Japan 2008)